The HUNDRED VERSES *of* ADVICE

Dilgo Khyentse Rinpoche

The
HUNDRED VERSES
of ADVICE

Tibetan Buddhist Teachings
on What Matters Most

DILGO KHYENTSE
&
PADAMPA SANGYE

Translated by the Padmakara Translation Group

SHAMBHALA
Boston &'London • 2006

Shambhala Publications, Inc.
Horticultural Hall
300 Massachusetts Avenue
Boston, Massachusetts 02115
www.shambhala.com

Printed in the United States of America

♾ This edition is printed on acid-free paper that meets the
American National Standards Institute z39.48 Standard.
♻ Shambhala Publications makes every effort to print on recycled paper.
For more information please visit www.shambhala.com.
Distributed in the United States by Random House, Inc.,
and in Canada by Random House of Canada Ltd

The Library of Congress catalogues the previous edition of this book as follows:

Rab-gsal-zla-ba, Dis-mgo Mkhyen-brtse, 1910–
The hundred verses of advice: Tibetan buddhist teachings on what matters most /
Dilgo Khyentse, Padampa Sangye; translated by the Padmakara Translation
Group.—1st Shambhala ed.
p. cm.
Based on: Padampa Sangye's renowned and inspiring poem was explained in 1987
by Dilgo Khyentse Rinpoche at Shechen Monastery in Nepal. Initially, Khyentse
Rinpoche was reading Padampa Sangye's verses from the Tingri edition of the root
text. Later, he sent for and switched to the Gdams ngag mdzod edition, which he
considered to be more reliable. These two editions are: 1. *Rje btsun dam pa sangs
rgyas kyis ding ri par zhal chems su stsal pa ding ri brgya rtsa ma,* in one hundred verses:
xylographic print in twelve folios from Tingri Langkhor, in western Tibet. 2. *Rgya
gar gyi grub thob chen po dam pa rgya gar ram dam pa sangs rgyas zhes pa'i gsung mgur
zhal gdams ding ri brgyad cu pa,* in eighty verses, pp. 31–36, vol. 13 of the *Gdams ngag
mdzod,* collected and edited by Jamgon Kongtrul Lodro Thaye (published by Lama
Ngodrup and Sherap Drimey, Paro, 1979, reprinted by Shechen Publications, Delhi,
2000). Includes bibliographical references.
ISBN 978-1-59030-154-8 (hardcover: alk. paper)
ISBN 978-1-59030-341-2 (paperback)
1. Dam-pa-saṅs-rgyas, d. 1117? Zal gdams Diṅ-ri bryga rtsa ma. 2. Mahayana
Buddhism—Doctrines. 3. Spiritual life—Buddhism—Doctrines. I. Dam-pa-saṅs-
rgyas, d. 1117? Zal gdams Diṅ-ri bryga rtsa ma. II. Title.
BQ7400.D353R25 2005
294.3'42042—dc22
2004016054

CONTENTS

Trulshik Rinpoche

FOREWORD

by Trulshik Rinpoche

OM SVASTI
Lion of the Word, who in the Holy Land and
* other places*
Assumed a human form and lived, for as long
As six hundred years, his wondrous life of
* liberation—*
To him, Sublime One, Long Life Vidyadhara,
* I respectfully bow down.*

To the people of Tingri in Tibet, the very
* words he spoke,*
The "Hundred Verses," profoundest of
* profound,*
Exquisitely adorning speech heard everywhere,
* and everywhere renowned,*

Are in this excellent book well clarified and
   truly well explained
By he who was the intentional reincarnate
   display
Of Jamyang Khyentse Wangpo, second
   Buddha of Tibet;
To him, Omniscient Unchanging Holder of
   the Supreme Vehicle Teachings
Whose adamantine tongue pronounced these
   words, I pay my heartfelt homage.

By way of an introduction to this book, following these opening verses, I would like to say a few words about the master known in the Holy Land of India as Acharya Kamalashila, and in Tibet as Padampa Sangye.

Padampa Sangye traveled to Tibet on three occasions for his first, middle, and final stay there, and we may confidently assume that in doing so he was guided by the Buddha in his primordial wisdom form. Indeed, he had a miraculous stone the Buddha had given him, and from India he hurled this stone toward Tibet, making the wish that wherever it fell he would there find disciples to train. He then left for Tibet in search of the stone.

It had fallen at a place now known as Tingri Langkhor, in Latö, in the province of Tsang. At the time Padampa Sangye arrived there, snow had been falling. But where the stone lay, he could see a darkened area where all the surrounding snow had melted. He was told that the stone, as it landed, had made the sound *ting*. The place was therefore called Tingri; and there Padampa founded his monastic seat at a site where musk deer walked around in a circle, and which thus became known as Lakor (or Langkhor), meaning "encircled by musk deer."

It was during his final visit to Tibet that Padampa met Lord Milarepa. The place where they came together and took part in a contest of miraculous powers is nowadays known as Nyingje Drönkhang, "Compassion Inn." This and other events are recounted in Jetsun Milarepa's autobiography.

Jamyang Khyentse Wangpo, holder of the Seven Transmissions, was an emanation of Acharya Kamalashila, alias Padampa Sangye; and Jamyang Khyentse Wangpo, in turn, chose to reappear as that magical Manifestation Body, mighty master of learning and accomplishment, guide of our mandala, the great banner of whose names—which I perforce must mention here—makes the whole world resplendent: Dilgo Khyentse Rinpoche, Gyurme Thekchok Tenpa Gyaltsen ("Victory Banner of the Unchanging Great Vehicle Doctrine"), Jigme Rabsel Dawa ("Fearless Brilliant Moon"). He it was who spoke this wonderful commentary, the text of which has been established, corrected, and translated into English and French by the Padmakara Translation Group in France. I most sincerely rejoice in this work, for it is of great importance that people from all walks of life, whether Buddhist or not, should read, study, and put into practice this excellent text.

Among the disciples of the sublime masters headed by the author of this work, this recommendation was written by the very worst, the Buddhist monk and ignoramus Ngawang Chökyi Lodrö, described as being the emanation of Dzarong Trulshik Shadeu. He made this prayer with folded hands on 8 December 1999, at Tashi Pelbar Ling in France. May virtue increase!

FOREWORD

by Khyentse Yangsi Rinpoche

The Hundred Verses of Advice, written by Padampa Sangye with commentary by my predecessor, Dilgo Khyentse Rinpoche, offers very powerful and practical teachings on how to solve the everyday problems that we may face in our jobs, schools, and relationships. It is not a book for Buddhist practitioners only, but for readers, young and old, from any background.

This book is a wake-up call that challenges us to look at ourselves and at the many possibilities that we have to change our own and others' lives for the better. It teaches us how to reach out to people who may need our help, as well as offers us answers to our spiritual inquiries.

Just glance through it and see for yourself. Read one or two pages at a time, then put it down and relax. Rest your mind on the words you just read. Think about the actual meaning of each sentence, each word, and each syllable. Once your mind improves, so will your health, and slowly, you will be better equipped to handle life's troubles.

The Hundred Verses of Advice is an accessible guide written using words that are clear, direct, and simple. There are no difficult practices, memorizations, or visualizations. It is easy for anybody to read and understand. It is my sincere prayer that this book will benefit and enrich the lives of all who come in contact with it.

Khyentse Yangsi Rinpoche
Boudhanath, Nepal
March 13, 2012

TRANSLATORS' NOTE

PADAMPA SANGYE'S RENOWNED and inspiring poem
was explained in 1987 by Dilgo Khyentse Rinpoche at
Shechen Monastery in Nepal, at the request of Matthieu Konchog Tendzin on behalf of Kunzang Dorje
and other disciples.

Initially, Khyentse Rinpoche was reading Padampa Sangye's verses from the Tingri edition of the
root text. Later, he sent for and switched to the *gdams
ngag mdzod* edition, which he considered to be more
reliable.

These two editions are:

1. *rje btsun dam pa sangs rgyas kyis ding ri par zhal
chems su stsal pa ding ri brgya rtsa ma*, in one hundred
verses: xylographic print in twelve folios from Tingri
Langkhor, in western Tibet.

2. *rgya gar gyi grub thob chen po dam pa rgya gar
ram dam pa sangs rgyas zhes pa'i gsung mgur zhal gdams
ding ri brgyad cu pa*, in eighty verses, pp. 31–36, vol. 13

of the *gdams ngag mdzod*, collected and edited by Jam-gön Kongtrul Lodrö Thaye (published by Lama Ngodrup and Sherap Drimey, Paro, 1979, reprinted by Shechen Publications, Delhi, 2000). Dilgo Khyentse Rinpoche's oral teachings were translated into English by Matthieu Ricard, and Padampa Sangye's written verses were translated by John Canti, both members of the Padmakara Translation Group.

We would like to express our gratitude to Lori and Fergus Flanagan, Michal Abrams, Matthew Akester, and Judith Amtzis for their help in improving the translation of the commentary, to John Canti for his masterful revision of it, and to Vivian Kurz for her work in all stages of the publication.

INTRODUCTION

As we approach the study of any spiritual teaching, we should begin by making the wish to attain enlightenment, not only for our personal liberation but also in order to be able to free all living beings from suffering and its causes, especially confusion and ignorance. Studying these instructions and putting them into practice will slowly allow us to realize this vast aspiration. Reflecting on the immense value of the teachings and conscious of how rare it is to have this opportunity, we should receive them with great attention and a humble, altruistic attitude, determined to make full use of them to the best of our ability.

The Hundred Verses of Advice is the spiritual testament of a great sage of India, Paramabuddha, better known under his Tibetan name, Padampa Sangye. In one of his past lives, he had been born as a close disciple of the Buddha, who foretold that in a future rebirth he would benefit an incalculable number of beings.

Thus he was reborn in the person of Padampa, meaning "sublime father" in Tibetan. A great scholar, he studied with 150 masters and put their teachings into practice until he truly became a treasury of spiritual knowledge. An accomplished yogi, he was graced by numerous visions and performed many miracles that bore witness to his spiritual realization. Finally, he attained the adamantine body, which transcends death and rebirth.

He traveled to China and Tibet three times, introducing the teachings of the "Pacification of Suffering," one of the eight great spiritual traditions of Tibet still practiced to this day.[1]

Padampa stayed for a long time in the high valley of Tingri, on the frontier between Tibet and Nepal. Among his innumerable disciples, four were particularly close to his heart. One day, one of these close students arrived in Tingri after a long absence and was so saddened to see how much the master had aged that he asked, "Sublime being, when you leave this world, you yourself, without doubt, will go from bliss to bliss; but what will become of us, the people of Tingri? In whom can we place our trust?"

For Padampa, dying would indeed be no more than passing from one Buddha-field to another. But for his disciples, his death would mean never again seeing his face or hearing his voice. "In a year's time," he said, "here you will find the corpse of an old Indian hermit."

Their eyes filled with tears, and it was for them that Padampa taught these Hundred Verses of Advice.

A year went by, and Padampa began to show signs of illness. When his disciples worried about his health, he told them laconically, "My mind is sick." To their perplexity, he added, "My mind has blended with the phenomenal world." He thus demonstrated that all dualistic perception had disappeared from his mind. "I do not know how to describe this type of disease," he added with a serene sense of humor. "Bodily ills can be treated, but this is incurable." He then fixed his gaze on the sky and passed away.

Statue of Padampa Sangye

The Verses and Commentary

> Homage to the teacher!
> Fortunate practitioners gathered here in
> Tingri, listen!

As a prelude to the teachings, Padampa Sangye pays homage to the spiritual master, the source of all blessings and the embodiment of all the buddhas of the past, present, and future. He considers the inhabitants of Tingri fortunate because they ardently wish to study and practice the Dharma, and have thus understood how to give meaning to their lives.

> Just as worn-out clothes can never again be
> made as new,
> It's no use seeing a doctor once you're
> terminally ill;
> You'll have to go. We humans living on this
> earth

> Are like streams and rivers flowing toward
>   the ocean—
> All living beings are heading for that single
>   destination.

Life exhausts itself day after day, second by second, like a piece of clothing that becomes threadbare over the years and eventually falls to pieces. Nothing and nobody can halt this ineluctable process. Illusory possessions like land and wealth are completely useless at the hour of death. In the end, leaving everything behind, we die alone, extracted from the familiar surroundings of our lives like a hair from a lump of butter.[2]

Our lives have no outcome other than death, just as rivers have no end other than the ocean. At the moment of death, our only recourse is spiritual practice, and our only friends the virtuous actions we have accomplished during our lifetime.

> Now, like a small bird flying off from a
>   treetop,
> I, too, will not be here much longer; soon I
>   must move on.

Nothing is more essential and precious than a spiritual teaching that can help us at the moment of death. The buddhas and spiritual teachers have bequeathed the living expression of their wisdom to us in the form of teachings. Such teachings, inseparable from those great beings themselves, allow anyone who takes them to heart to attain their level of realization and provide a constant source of inspiration to those on the path of liberation.

1

*If you spend the present meaninglessly and
leave with empty hands,
People of Tingri, a human life in future will
be very hard to find.*

Some people feel that there is no hurry to meet a
spiritual master and that there will always be time
in the future to practice the Dharma. With this attitude, you will neglect spiritual practice in favor of the
pursuit of your ordinary preoccupations.

When the season for sowing comes, farmers start
work immediately. They do not postpone their task
until the next day. In the same way, when favorable
conditions for practicing the Dharma come together,
you need to focus all your energy on practice, without
further delay. ॐ

2

*To apply yourselves with body, speech, and
mind to the sacred teachings,
People of Tingri, is the best thing you can do.*

Through the unfailing process of cause and effect, our acts, our words, and our thoughts determine the happiness or the suffering that we will later experience. If the balance of our acts leans to the negative side, we will suffer in the lower states of existence of samsara. If it leans toward the positive, we will be able to liberate ourselves from samsara and attain Buddhahood in a single lifetime. The choice is clear: avoid the causes of sorrow and thus be sure of happiness.

If you are born as a human being, in a place where Buddhism has flourished, and you meet an accomplished spiritual master, you can put his instructions into practice and reap immense benefits in this life and in all future lives. You will realize that your focus on worldly distractions and preoccupations is holding you prisoner in samsara, and you will begin to feel an intense desire to free yourself. Right now, you are at the crossroads: one way leads to liberation, the other to the different realms of samsara.

A sutra says:

> The body is the boat that can lead you to the
>   shore of liberation,
> The body is the stone that can make you
>   sink into the abysses of samsara,
> The body is the servant of vice and of virtue.

Just as a pure crystal refracts the color of whatever it is placed on, your acts become negative or positive according to your intention. It is therefore essential that you take the right path and direct your acts, words, and thoughts toward the Dharma.

In the beginning, you need to concentrate all your energies on cultivating positive tendencies and eliminating negative ones. The Brahmin Upagupta, who lived during the time of the Buddha, used to sharpen his vigilance and measure his progress by keeping a daily account. Every evening, he would make two heaps of stones, using a black pebble for each bad thought or action he had committed during the day and a white stone for each meritorious one. At first, the heap of black pebbles would be much higher, but little by little, the two heaps became equal. With great perseverance, he eventually reached a point where all the stones he piled up were white. ❧

3

*Give your very life, heart, and soul to the
    Three Jewels,
People of Tingri, and their blessings cannot
    but arise.*

Unshakable confidence in the Three Jewels, and
in the spiritual master who embodies them, is
like a calm and clear lake, in which the moon of their
blessings is clearly reflected. When you have the strength
of such confidence, your mind remains serene and imperturbable, graced with the presence of the Three
Jewels. What do good or bad circumstances matter to
you then? ॐ

4

*Forget your goals for this life—concentrate
instead on lives to come.
People of Tingri, that is the highest goal.*

I t would be futile to practice the Dharma only
within the narrow perspective of this life, with your
own health, longevity, and comfort as your main goals.
Instead, think hard about what is going to happen to
you in all your lives to come. And it is not only your
own future you must consider, but that of all beings,
too. Whatever you do, it is the underlying intention
that determines whether the result is positive or negative. If you are going to master and transform your
mind—which is, after all, the goal of the Dharma—it
is important that you start by examining those underlying intentions and thoughts. Are you really practicing the Dharma for your own good, or for that of
others?

Our first concern tends to be our own search for happiness and our attempts to escape suffering. But if you step back and see yourself as just one among the whole infinity of sentient beings, your individual wants and fears begin to look insignificant in comparison. Just as you want to be happy, so too does every single one of all those beings. But in their pursuit of happiness, almost everything they do only results in suffering. If only they could hear and follow the profound teaching of the Dharma, then, like the blind recovering their sight, they would see that happiness—for oneself and others, in this life and in lives to come—is brought about solely by positive actions. The only way to get free of the vicious circle of suffering and to attain the lasting happiness of enlightenment is to pay careful attention to undertaking positive actions and avoiding negative ones. Indeed, if you yourself have not fully assimilated this truth, you may claim to wish to help others, but your efforts will all be in vain.

When you are following the teachings and putting them into practice, this is why it is so important to do so not with ideas of being respected or rewarded for your great learning, but with the thought "May I attain enlightenment and be able to give these teachings to all beings, thus leading them to Buddhahood."

If your mind is oriented toward such positive goals, you can be sure that the words you speak and the actions you perform, like servants taking their cue from their master, will naturally follow in the same direction.

But if your mind is distracted and full of attachment, animosity, and ignorance, then however many millions of mantras you recite or prostrations you offer, it will be like eating tasty food mixed with poison. That is not the way to progress toward Buddhahood.

Try to maintain perfectly pure thoughts in all circumstances, so that even the most insignificant of your acts will preserve their positive energy until you attain enlightenment. A drop of water that falls into the ocean will last as long as the ocean itself. ॐ

5

Families are as fleeting as a crowd on market day;
People of Tingri, don't bicker or fight.

Family ties are as ephemeral as a chance meeting in the marketplace. In the course of my long life, I have more than once witnessed difficulties between husbands and wives, parents and children. Large families are often the scene of strong attachments and hatred, which can all too easily give rise to disputes and resentment. When the winds of trouble blow on a family, tensions that may have begun with a few momentary hostile or possessive thoughts can end up driving some of its members, as if possessed by a demon, to kill each other or commit suicide.

When a man and a woman have come together through the force of their karma, they should try to live in harmony. There is nothing good about quarrels—they cause great suffering for everyone involved.

Make it your responsibility to be agreeable to all the members of your family, and to try to turn their minds little by little toward the Dharma, simply through kindness and setting a good example.

Large numbers of monks and nuns live communally in the monasteries. It is essential that they feel united and maintain excellent discipline. Harmonious monastic communities are the very foundation of Dharma.

The same is true of the relationship between teacher and disciple. If the students can maintain a perfectly pure relationship with their teacher (these spiritual ties are called *samaya* in Sanskrit), they will not stumble against any obstacle on the path.

Many of us have crossed the threshold of the Adamantine Vehicle and have received initiations from the same spiritual master, at the heart of the same mandala. Thus we have become spiritual brothers and sisters, and any discord or dispute between us is a grave mistake. It is said that if a dispute breaks out between participants in the great Vajrayana ceremony called a *drupchen*, in that instant the whole long ritual is entirely spoiled, just as when a rat falls into a milk churn, all the milk is rendered undrinkable. ❧

6

*Wealth and property, like a magic show, just
seduce and deceive;
People of Tingri, don't let the knot of
avarice bind you.*

Vast wealth, the finest clothing and food—even if
you had everything you could ever want, there is
no way those possessions could last forever. Whatever
is accumulated will inevitably one day be exhausted.
Whatever goods and property you may amass, all of it
will sooner or later be dispersed. Power and high posi-
tions are no different, for whatever rises must fall. No
one has held the same rank forever. All gatherings,
too, are bound to end in separation; a hundred thousand people may be assembled, only to be separated a
few hours later. Life itself is transitory, and birth inevitably ends in death. Has there ever lived a single being
safe from death?

Someone who has managed to build up a great fortune may look back at his achievements with some satisfaction, reflecting proudly, "I am a rich man." But he would do well to reflect, too, on the extent to which those riches are based on lies, deceit, and the overriding of others' interests—negative actions that in the long run will only engender suffering.

There is nothing intrinsically wrong with wealth, if it is acquired honestly and used for constructive ends. It can be put to good use to relieve poverty, to make offerings to the Three Jewels, and to sustain the monastic community and people in need. Those who benefit from the generosity of benefactors should use the sustenance they receive without any greed, for the sole aim of pursuing their spiritual practice. Both donor and recipient should stay free of attachment and consider their "possessions" as illusory gifts received in a dream. Just as wealth itself from an ultimate point of view has no real existence, the merit you can accumulate by using it with generosity is also insubstantial and unreal. It can nonetheless lead you to Buddhahood, one aspect of which is freedom from any grasping onto phenomena.

Once you fall under the sway of avarice, however, your hands are tied and your mind is closed. You not only lose the ability to give, you even begin to find other people's generosity unbearable. This attitude creates the conditions for rebirth among *preta*s, spirits who are constantly tortured by hunger and thirst.

Powerful attachment can even lead to the experience of intense suffering in the hell realms. During the time of the Buddha, there was a monk who owned a beautiful alms bowl to which he was strongly attached. When he died, even before his body was cremated, he was reborn in the form of a venomous serpent. No sooner was the serpent born than it made its way to the monk's bowl, coiled up inside, and hissed menacingly at all who approached. This incident was reported to the Buddha, who explained where the serpent had come from. With words of truth,[3] the Buddha exhorted the snake to abandon its negative concepts. At once, the creature left the bowl and fled into the forest. Its attachment and hatred remained so strong, however, that flames came from its mouth. It died and was instantaneously reborn in the fires of hell. At the same instant, the funeral pyre of the former monk was lit, so that three fires burned at once. That unfortunate monk was nicknamed "He who burned three times."

The terrible pangs of hunger and thirst felt by the *preta*s can be relieved by the offering of water *tormas*[4] in the morning and the smoke of burning food in the evening, especially when these offerings are made with great compassion.

Love and nonattachment are the basis of true generosity. We ought to be generous, and give as much as we can to those in need. ❧

7

This body is just a bag containing various kinds of filth;
People of Tingri, don't pamper it and spruce it up so.

"I look better than anyone else around," a pretty woman may think, "and I can attract and charm anyone I want." But her beautiful body is actually just blood, fat, muscle, lymph, bones, and excrement, nothing good or pleasant! The human body is like a vase of fine porcelain full of excrement. Open it, and you will feel nauseous.

What a waste of time it is to take so much care of this body, feeding it the most succulent dishes, dressing it in the most fashionable clothes, and trying to make it look younger than it really is. The body has no other destination than the cemetery where it will be burned, buried, or fed to the birds.

Impelled by the vainest of motives, we plunge into business and compete with our rivals without hesitating to lie and to cheat, thus adding the weight of negative actions to the futility of our goals. Nor are we ever finally satisfied. Our wealth is not great enough, our food is not good enough, and our pleasures never seem to be sufficiently intense.

What more do you need, if you have enough food and clothing to sustain your life and protect you from the elements? Our spiritual teachers were content with that. They never coveted luxurious clothing or costly and refined dishes, and they laughed at comfort and fame.

The importance we ordinarily accord our body, therefore, is scarcely merited. But as a tool with which to practice the Dharma, its value is inestimable. Unfortunately, it is a tool we only have for a short period of time—until we die. Instead of just giving it as much pleasure and comfort as we can, we must put it to good use, to progress toward enlightenment.

If you cannot free yourself from being so obsessed by your body, your attachment and negative emotions can only increase. Consider the body as an illusion, a form in a dream. Give it whatever care is needed to keep it in good health, and devote all your attention to spiritual practice. In this way, you will one day become like the bodhisattvas, who no longer have the slightest attachment to their bodies, and are ready to give their limbs, their eyes, even their lives, if that can benefit others. ❧

8

*Family and friends are no more real than a
magic show;
People of Tingri, in your fondness for them
don't tie yourself down.*

Simply to see our friends and family makes us
happy. As soon as we hear our child cry, we are
seized by anxiety. Such feelings dominate our mind
and lead it astray. Throughout our life, we hang on
to those close to us and fear their death as well as our
own. We might sometimes think of going into the
mountains to devote ourselves completely to Dharma
practice in solitary retreat, but then we hesitate, thinking, "Who will take care of my family, my business,
my fields?" and we keep postponing any such decision.
Even when our last breath comes, our mind is still too
obsessed with our loved ones for us to face death with
serenity and pray to be reborn in a Buddha-field.

The best way to reaffirm your determination is to

consider those close to you and all your possessions, as well as everything else in the world around you, as being a magical show without any true, substantial existence. A magician knows that the birds and horses he has conjured up are apparitions without any reality, so he does not get attached to them—but he can still relate to them and enjoy their presence.

Many of us lead family lives. At most, the members of a family stay together for the duration of a lifetime, often much less. While that fleeting moment of being together still lasts, we should try to remain in perfect harmony with each other, while observing the Dharma as much as possible. Night and day, let us turn our minds toward goodness, love, and compassion. Doing a single prostration, saying a simple prayer, contemplating the nature of the mind for an instant are seeds that lead to enlightenment. To be united in this life as man and wife, parents and children, is the result of our past actions, of a shared karma. That is why we should at all costs avoid quarreling and live in harmony.

And those of you who are capable of renouncing a family lifestyle for the monastic life should pray that, once you attain enlightenment, your friends and those close to you will be the first disciples whom you lead on the road to liberation. ❧

9

*Country and land are like a nomad's
pastures;
People of Tingri, don't cling sentimentally
to them.*

We call the country in which we were born our homeland. In truth, however, there is nowhere among the six realms of samsara that is not our homeland, because we have been born so many times, in so many places. Like nomads moving camp every season, we change our native land with every rebirth. What is the point of getting attached to one country rather than another? ৯৯

10

*As parents, all beings in the six realms have
cared for you;
People of Tingri, don't relate to them with
your ideas of "I" and "mine."*

We share with all beings the fatherland of the six realms (see note 5). At one point or another, throughout all of your infinite past lives, every single being has been your mother, your father, your friend, or your enemy. What, therefore, is the point of discriminating between the friends you happen to like and the enemies you want to get rid of just now, within the narrow confines of this present life? These rigid and limited concepts of friend and enemy feed a torrent of attachments and hatreds that obscure the mind.

By sticking to notions of "I" and "mine" and blindly following the feelings of attraction and repulsion to which these notions give rise, we accumulate negative karma. Let us stop doing that! ॐ

11

*The day you were born, your death began
approaching;
People of Tingri, remember: there is never
any time to spare.*

The birth of a baby is considered the most joyful of
events. Yet nothing can halt that child's relentless
course toward death. Whatever different directions he
or she may take during life, there is no way to be
spared from death. The proverb says: "As the sun goes
further in its course, the shadows of the western
mountains draw ever closer; so too, as life unfolds its
course, is death forever drawing nearer."

The child, growing into adolescence, still thinks
that he has plenty of time. What a mistake! It is sense-
less to constantly put things off until later. The hour
of death can strike at any moment. Each breath is one
more movement toward death, just like the steps of an
animal being led to the slaughterhouse.

Your present life is just one life; future lives are innumerable. Do not sacrifice so many lives just to pursue the illusory well-being of this present one. If you neglect to practice Dharma day after day, you will regret it bitterly—but too late, at the moment of death. Can a dying person begin to practice? Right now is the time to devote yourself to spiritual practice. The experience that practice will bring you is the only thing that will help you at the hour of death. ✿

12

Fundamentally there's no delusion, it's an
ephemeral occurrence;
People of Tingri, look at the nature of what
produces it.

However much you may wash and scrub a lump of coal, you will never manage to make it white. Now, we could imagine that ignorance was part of our intrinsic nature, like the blackness of coal. If this were so, ignorance and delusion would be impossible to eliminate. In fact, ignorance and delusion have no true existence at all and thus cannot alter in any way our true, intrinsic nature—the Buddha-nature. It is as fundamentally pure and unalterable as gold. At most, it can be masked for a while by ignorance, but its essence does not change.

Ignorance takes form temporarily, under certain conditions, like a cloud in the sky. For a while, a cloud forms an imposing white mass that obscures the brilliance of the sun. But if we fly toward this cloud and enter it, we find it is impalpable. It did not exist before, and it will eventually vanish into thin air. As for the sun, it has never changed and is completely unaffected by the cloud.

The veils ignorance creates are contingent, ephemeral, and ungraspable. They do not alter or affect our primordial nature, and are not a part of it. Ignorance, the root of all delusion, lures beings into samsara. But however solid it may seem, it has never had so much as an atom of reality. Since it has never been born, it can never exist, much less cease to exist. When the realization of emptiness dissipates the veils of ignorance, the natural qualities of Buddhahood are revealed. The sun, which has never ceased to shine, appears as soon as the wind blows away the clouds. ❧

13

Without distraction apply yourselves to the
sacred Dharma;
People of Tingri, after death it will guide
you on the path.

The flowering of youth showers us with health
and strength, and makes us want to enjoy life
intensely. With unabated enthusiasm, we endeavor in
every possible way to increase our fortune and our
power. For some, succeeding in their own aims may
well involve hurting others to do so. However, at the
moment of death we will realize the futility of all these
preoccupations and feverish activities. But by then,
alas, it is too late to go back.

Great beauty cannot get the better of death by se-
duction, great wealth cannot bribe it away, and the
greatest strength or power cannot force it to wait even
for an instant. The most powerful head of state must
in his turn obey death's call. Death will disarm the

general, regardless of the powerful arsenal at his disposal. Only the spiritual experience acquired in the course of our lives can help us at the moment of death.

Quick! Let us practice before old age ravages our physical and intellectual faculties. Let us turn our back on the delusion and childish distractions of ordinary life and devote ourselves to the practice of the Dharma. Then, at the moment of death, as the unequaled Gampopa said, "In the best case, we will realize the absolute nature, the *dharmakaya* (see note 9). In the middle case, certain of being reborn in a Buddha-field, we will be filled with joy, like a child returning home. In the worst of cases, we will have no regret, because we have encountered a spiritual master and practiced his instructions." Let us prepare ourselves, from this very moment onward, and at the moment of death we will be able to apply the teachings we have received. ❧

14

*The truth of cause and effect ensures that
actions yield their full result;
People of Tingri, avoid all actions that are
negative and evil.*

I f dying simply meant that we disappeared like
water absorbed into dry ground or like a flame
being extinguished, we could take death quite lightly.
But this is not the case. We abandon our body; but we
keep our mind, which travels in the state of transition
between death and rebirth, called the *bardo*.[5]

In this state, where we have no material body, we
cannot use our five senses in the ordinary way. Death
has extracted us from the company of our family and
friends like a hair pulled out of a lump of butter.[6] But
there is one thing we have brought with us, and which
stays with us as closely as a shadow—the actions we
have done in the past. If negative actions weigh heav-
ier, we are not going to be able to escape the torments

of the lower realms of samsara. On the contrary, if positive actions predominate, we are going to be reborn in a higher state of existence and will be able to continue to progress toward liberation. As our mind travels through the ever-changing experience of the bardo, we cannot choose to do what seems good to us, or take our time to decide what direction to take. There is no way out. Like a feather in the wind, we are driven by the force of our past actions, dragged along by the soldiers of death. We have no moment of respite in which to pull ourselves together. We cannot stay anywhere or leave at will. Tossed hither and thither, our mental body does not obey us.

It is crucial to understand and to gain the conviction that the laws of cause and effect govern the universe and all beings. Milarepa explained that if he had been able to dedicate himself totally to Dharma and attain enlightenment in a single lifetime, it was simply because of the conviction he had in the laws of karma. Every action inevitably has a result. The traces of our positive or harmful actions dwell in the substratum of our consciousness. There are only two ways to erase the trace left by a harmful act: either by going through the experience of suffering that is its natural consequence, or by purifying it with the appropriate antidotes before the appearance of its dire effects.

When the spiritual master tells us that all our positive and negative acts are sure to cause their inevitable consequences, we hear his words; but we do not really believe him. If we did, we would never dare to carry out even the least harmful of negative actions, and we would place great importance on developing positive actions, even the most insignificant. Do we not value a nugget of gold, no matter how small? ❧

15

Leave all your activities behind like a country in a dream;
People of Tingri, just put nonaction into practice.

The various activities of ordinary life follow one after another like the waves of the ocean. The rich never feel they have enough money; the powerful never feel they have enough power. Think about it: the best way to satisfy all your desires and complete all your projects is to abandon them.

A realized being sees the preoccupations of ordinary people as being like the events in a dream, and watches them like an old man watching children play. Last night you dreamed, perhaps, of being a great king, but when you woke up, what was left? What you experience in the waking state has scarcely more reality than that. Rather than pursuing these elusive dreams, let your mind rest in serene contemplation, free of mental agitation and distraction, until the realization of emptiness becomes an integral part of your experience. ❧

16

The very thing you feel attached to, let go of
it, whatever—
People of Tingri, there isn't anything you
need.

T hink of any person, any object or situation about
which you feel strong grasping or possessiveness,
and try to look clearly at the beauty, power, or wealth
to which you are so attached. Examine each of them
down to the very foundation. Do they not seem like
illusions? When you look at things in this way, your
attachments diminish and you no longer feel the same
pressing need to possess them. If you take the attitude
"I don't need anything!" your state of mind will be
naturally free and serene.

On the other hand, if you live and die in a state of
intense attachment, your present existence and your
lives to come will be tormented. Someone who dies

with strong concern for the possessions he leaves behind will become a spirit tortured by avarice.

The great saints and practitioners of the past contented themselves with the minimum amount of food necessary to stay alive, and with just enough clothes to protect them from the cold. Yet they were the richest of all, because true wealth belongs to those who know how to be content with what they have. Karak Gomchung, a great Kadampa meditator, lived in a cave in Tibet. A hawthorn bush obstructed the entrance and caught on the hermit's robe each time he entered and left. He often considered cutting the bush, but then immediately the thought of death would arise in his mind, and he would think, "Who knows when I'll die? The time it took to get rid of this thorn bush would be better spent in meditation." By the power of his meditation, Karak Gomchung was able to fly and perform all kinds of miracles. And when he died, the bush was still there.

If such great practitioners cannot bear to squander even a single moment, how can we, who have so much yet to accomplish on the spiritual path, waste most of our lives in ordinary activities? ❧

17

*Since you won't be staying in this world
    forever,
People of Tingri, make your preparations for
    the journey now.*

Which of us has not thought of building our-
    selves a house that we can live in for many
decades, and that will last for centuries after we have
gone? Which of us has not dreamed of making a fortune and being free from all worries for the rest of
our lives? This "demon of eternity" beguiles us into
believing things can last forever.

But the belief that anything or anyone could be
ours forever is one that is bound to be disappointed.
How tragic it is to see people on their deathbed, so
distraught at the thought of leaving their loved ones
behind, so preoccupied with their possessions, and with
their final testament—which in truth is little more
than a list of their attachments—but so blind to the

fate that awaits them, which is likely to be a tormented one if they have so completely neglected anything truly meaningful. And, by contrast, how inspiring it is to hear about or meet those wise and authentic practitioners who do not feel that they own anything at all, not even their bodies, much less any material objects or places they may live in. Whatever possessions they may have, they see as unreal and illusory, momentarily on loan.

We have a long journey to make through the six realms of samsara. We should approach the Dharma like a sailor making his meticulous preparations for a voyage around the world, and prepare ourselves properly for our far longer journey, through death and rebirth. ॐ

18

*If first you finish what you have to do, you'll
never get to Dharma;
People of Tingri, while you're thinking of it,
practice straight away.*

The activities of ordinary life are never-ending,
like the ripples of water on the surface of a lake.
You might think that you will be able to conclude all
your projects during the next ten or twenty years, and
that after that you will be able to practice the Dharma
with your mind at ease. But surely you are ignoring
the fragility of life. Have you not seen people die
young in all sorts of unforeseeable ways? It is unrea-
sonable to assume that nothing of the sort can ever
happen to you.

If the thought of practicing the Dharma occurs to
you, do not hesitate for a moment. Do not just put it
off until tomorrow. The right moment is now. The
farmer does not wait for frost to harden the ground

before sowing his fields. He does it when the soil is warm and moist. As soon as you have met a qualified spiritual teacher and have received the teacher's instructions, you are ready to set out on the path of awakening. ❧

19

*Inside the forest, monkeys may be living
happily at ease,
People of Tingri—but at the edges forest
fires are closing in all around.*

Fires may surround a forest, but deep in the heart
of the woods the monkeys are leaping casually
from branch to branch, frolicking and enjoying delicious fruits. They do not know that soon they will be
burned alive by the flames that encircle them. Like-
wise, the proud, the powerful, and the rich amuse
themselves in life, as if unaware that death is about to
ambush them and cut them down. Reflect on what
really counts at the instant of death, and follow the
path to enlightenment, which is the only intelligent
way to use your life. ॐ

20

*Birth, sickness, aging, and death flow on, a
river without ford or bridge;
People of Tingri, have you prepared
yourselves a boat?*

Birth, sickness, aging, and death are the four great
torments of humankind. Birth is the threshold of
life and also the threshold of suffering. Soon age will
impair our health, weaken our senses, make our teeth
fall out, and turn our hair white. Loss of memory will
make us cantankerous; nobody wants to listen to grumpy
old people. Anxiety will never stop tormenting us. What
will become of our possessions and our affairs? We
worry about how our children will neglect them all. Illness, too, brings its burden of afflictions. Withered and
in pain, we will finally have to face the agony of death.

These four great trials form a tumultuous river
that all of us must cross. Had we not better start right
now preparing the vessel that will permit us to reach
the other shore? ৯

21

In the narrow defiles of birth, death, and the
intermediate state,
Bandits await—the five poisonous
emotions—sure to ambush you;
People of Tingri, avail yourselves of the
teacher as your escort.

Traveling on paths that pass through regions infested by bandits is a fearful experience fraught
with dangers. The spiritual path, too, leads through
difficult and dangerous defiles, and anyone making the
arduous journey toward enlightenment must expect to
encounter some formidable obstacles, especially desire,
anger, confusion, pride, and jealousy. You may manage
to avoid the ambush set up by desire, only to find anger
lying in wait, ready to overpower you at the next crossroads on your path. Even if you escape that danger, it
will be all too easy to fall into the clutches of pride and
jealousy. The five poisonous emotions are merciless

marauders who will not have the slightest hesitation in killing your chance of reaching your destination, freedom from samsara. To bring you through these dangers, you will need a soundly reliable escort. That escort is the spiritual master. Only with the master's guidance will you arrive safe and sound.

As there is so much at stake, begin by choosing a truly qualified spiritual master. Once you have established confidence in the master, listen to the teacher's advice. And finally, learn how to put it into practice. If you can follow these three stages correctly, you will progress quickly and without obstacles. Thanks to the kindness and wisdom of the spiritual teacher, the whole of the Dharma is available to you, set out like a display of sumptuous foods in the marketplace. Would it not be foolish of you to miss this chance?

If you put your confidence in an authentic spiritual master, you will have one practice to apply when you get old, another when you fall ill, and another at the threshold of death. You will be ready to face life and death with resolute confidence. ॐ

22

*Your never-failing source of refuge is the
teacher;
People of Tingri, carry him constantly on
the crown of your head.*

No matter what circumstances arise, the compassionate kindness of the spiritual teacher will never forsake you. If you put your confidence in the teacher, he will guide you until enlightenment. The stronger your confidence, the faster your spiritual development will unfold; and if you can truly see your teacher as the Buddha in person, your progress on the path will be very swift.

How should you follow a teacher? More important than material offerings is to serve the teacher with your body, speech, and mind. And, above all, repay the teacher's kindness by putting the teachings into practice with great endeavor.

How do you start out on the path? First receive

instructions from your teacher, then make sure that you understand their meaning, and finally integrate them into your being.

How should you practice these instructions? Be like a hungry yak, browsing on one tuft of grass with its eyes already fixed on the next. Practice with joy and enthusiasm, and never fall into laziness or apathy. Especially, never think "Now that is enough." People start to feel proud of themselves after offering a few thousand prostrations and reciting a few hundred thousand mantras, while at the same time feeling not the slightest hesitation to kill insects, indulge all their whims, and make light of their negative acts, numerous though these may be. That is a big mistake. And that is why we need the guidance of a spiritual teacher just as much as a young child needs the guidance of its parents.

Try to bring all your experience into the context of devotion to the teacher. If you can grasp this vital point of the practice, you will have no obstacles. If your situation is pleasant and easy, see your happiness, without any attachment, as the blessings of the teacher, and as a dream, an illusion. And if you go through difficulties and suffering, see that, too, as the blessings of the teacher. If you fall ill, visualize your spiritual teacher wherever it is in your body that you feel pain or that is the site of the disease. Recognize that illness and pain offer you an opportunity to purify yourself of harmful past actions and of ignorance—the sources of suffer-

ing. Keep in mind the many other beings who are suffering in the same way as you are, and pray that your
suffering may absorb theirs, and that they may be liberated from all suffering. In this way, illness can teach
us compassion. ❧

23

*If your protection is the teacher, you'll reach
wherever you aspire to go;
People of Tingri, cultivate devotion as the
fare you pay for the journey.*

The spiritual master is like the earth, never giving
way beneath our feet. The spiritual master leads
us to enlightenment without disappointing us. Borne
by the air, a plane can take us quickly to where we
could never go on foot. Borne by our devotion, the
blessings of the teacher bring us swiftly to realization.

One of the meanings of the word *dharma* is "that
which holds." It holds and guides those who give
themselves to it with confidence. A person being swept
away by the swift current of a river can be gripped by
a firm hand and hauled on to the bank. In the same
way, the teacher's hook can pull us out of the round of
deaths and rebirths, as long as we can hold out to him
the ring of our faith.

No student at any level of teaching in Buddhism, from the Fundamental Vehicle up to the Great Perfection, can do without the guidance of an authentic spiritual master. To place our trust in such a teacher is the best way to progress and to avert all the potential hindrances and wrong turnings that we could encounter. So, on our journey toward enlightenment, devotion is the fare—it is what we have to contribute ourselves in order to reach our destination. ✖

24

Those who get wealthy get miserly, too;
People of Tingri, give generously without
being partial.

It is said that "the richer people get, the more miserly they are," and this saying is often true. Avarice makes you unhappy. It exposes you to rebirth in the form of tortured spirits. Rather than store useless riches, use them in a constructive way. Be generous toward those in need, build stupas, and make offerings to the Three Jewels. The more generous you are, the more you will prosper.

Generosity should always be exercised impartially toward all—the poor, the sick, the aged, the traveler from afar—without discrimination between friend and stranger, between those on whom we count and those from whom we can expect nothing. In giving, be free of ostentation, of favoritism, and of any expectation of reward. ৯

25

Whoever gets power acts sinfully, too;
People of Tingri, abandon all desire for rank
and power.

To establish their authority, heads of state often resort to negative acts. They are responsible for the offenses committed in their name, and they will harvest the results. The leader of an army will ultimately experience the result created by each death caused by the soldiers under his command.

What is the benefit of power built upon so many misdeeds? Why thirst for power, for wealth, for an elevated rank and social position, when these things can never last and attract only suffering? The only position from which you can never fall is the awakened state. ॐ

26

Those with rank and riches are never happy
and at ease;
People of Tingri, get ready to claw at your
chest in anguish.

No one is more agitated and anxious than the person who thinks money is everything. "How am I going to make my fortune? Then, how am I going to hold on to it?" He lives in constant fear of thieves, competitors, and catastrophes. When he ends up losing his wealth, he feels as if his own flesh were being cut off.

Look at how some people rush about night and day for the sake of their business or their career, wearing themselves out in the pursuit of success and the effort of preventing setbacks. They are suspicious of everyone and are constantly attempting to profit from their inferiors, outmatch their equals, and oust their superiors. They hardly ever enjoy a carefree, untroubled moment.

What a simple joy it is not to have power or position in society and to have nothing to lose and nothing to fear!

Do not encumber your mind with useless thoughts. What good is it to brood over the past and fret about the future? Dwell in the simplicity of the present moment. Live in harmony with the Dharma. Make it the heart of your life and experience. Be the master of your destiny. ॐ

27

*In the next world, there are neither family
nor friends;
People of Tingri, place your confidence in
the Dharma.*

We cry out with pain from the prick of a tiny thorn and shudder at the touch of icy water, but this body, which we cherish so much, will soon be a corpse without any feeling at all. Its only future is to be burned, buried, devoured by dogs, or torn apart by vultures. When we leave this world, neither our parents, children, and friends, nor our servants, houses, and wealth will go with us. Like a feather, we will be carried off by the wind of karma. Where will we go? Where will we stay? We will no longer have any choice.

Who will be able to help us? We can only rely with confidence on the spiritual teacher, the Three Jewels, and the Dharma that we have practiced in our lifetime, for only they have the power to liberate us from the

torments and terrors of the intermediate state between
death and rebirth, and to guide us toward the Buddha-
fields.

The Dharma begins with difficulties but culmi-
nates in bliss. It is very different from ordinary worldly
involvement, which begins with joy and ends in dis-
tress and disillusionment.

What difficult trials and austerities Milarepa had
to endure! However, it is through them that he attained the unchanging level of Vajradhara, the pure
bliss of nonduality. He lived in lonely caves, but his
glory traveled throughout the world. He, too, had to
cross the door of death, but now he sits at the center
of the mandala of the Land of Pure Joy. How different
from the proud people of this world! When a head of
state or a millionaire dies, people say, "So-and-so is
dead." That is all—nothing more significant than a
blown-out candle, a puddle of water evaporated.

The word *dharma* also means "to amend" or "to
correct." To correct all imperfections and develop all
perfections—how else can we win freedom? The qualities that result from the practice of Dharma remain
with us as a spiritual potential for our future lives. ❧

28

If you wander in distraction, you'll waste the freedoms and advantages of human life; People of Tingri, make a resolute decision now.

If there is one constant tendency of our fickle and ever-changing minds, it is our strong predilection for ordinary distractions. Until we learn to master our thoughts and attain true stability of mind, our commitment is bound to be hesitant and we run the risk of being distracted by activities with little true meaning, wasting our life and the precious opportunities for the Dharma it has brought us. To postpone the practice of Dharma until tomorrow is tantamount to postponing it till we die.

Moved by faith, the hunter Chirawa Gonpo Dorje told Milarepa, "I have decided to take up the Dharma. But first I have to go back home to take leave of my family. I will return immediately afterward."

The hermit cut him short: "Make up your mind now. If you return home, your family will try to make you change your mind, and you will not return. If you intend to concentrate on the Dharma, decide to do it right now." So that is exactly what Gonpo Dorje did, and he became one of Milarepa's most realized disciples.

Do not fall into the trap of hesitation! Focus all your energy and devote yourself to practice, without letting any other consideration interfere with that. ❧

29

While you're busy being distracted, the
demon of death will catch you;
People of Tingri, practice from this very
moment onward.

Your fields need to be worked, or your business needs to be attended to, or your search for a suitable partner may be your main concern—I can only guess at the things you spend your time on. But remember, the more your life is taken up by such concerns, the more you run the risk of death robbing you of what little time you set aside for Dharma practice. Do not allow the weight of ordinary preoccupations to divert you from the pursuit of Dharma. If the thought of practicing occurs to you one day, start that very day. If it comes one night, start that very night. Whatever the place and the time, do it there and then. ॐ

30

When will the demon of death appear?
There is no way to tell;
People of Tingri, right now be always on
your guard.

Death is as sudden and decisive as lightning. It strikes without warning, no matter what the circumstances.

You could be in good health, enjoying a delicious meal with friends, or contemplating a beautiful landscape. Yet, at that very moment, death could be only a few seconds away. Those close to you will be left behind, your conversation will be left unfinished, your meal will be left uneaten, your projects left uncompleted.

Does it not happen all the time that people suddenly die, victims of an accident, murdered, poisoned by contaminated food or by the wrong medicine, injured in a game or sport, or killed in war? Death is always lurking nearby, an ever-present menace. Be constantly on your guard, like a traveler going through a country infested with bandits. A political leader threatened with assassination never relaxes his vigilance; he avoids sleeping two successive nights in the same place, always aware of the imminence of death. Be like that all the time. Every night, go to sleep thinking, "In the morning, will they find a corpse in my bed?" ❧

31

The day you die, there's no one who'll
protect you;
People of Tingri, be ready to have yourselves
alone to count on.

When you reach the threshold of death, the friends and relatives around you have no way of accompanying you any further. There is very little they can do to help you at all. Not even the richest magnate can take a penny of his wealth with him, and it would be in vain that even the most powerful of generals ordered his troops to keep death at bay—like everyone else, he will just have to surrender.

Your consciousness will leave your body and wander in the bardo. There, with an illusory mental body, you will find yourself alone in the shadows, lost and desperate, not knowing what to do, not knowing where to go. The hallucinations that torment most beings at that time are terrifying beyond description. Although they are no more than projections of the mind, they nevertheless have a powerful reality at the time.

The only possible source of comfort will be the experience you may have acquired through practicing the Dharma. That is why it is so important to make the effort to practice now. Even in times of peace, a nation foresees the eventuality of war and remains ready to respond. In the same way, stay on the alert, and prepare yourself for death by practicing the Dharma. Like an eternal harvest, it will keep you supplied with provisions for the life to come and will be the very basis of your future happiness. ❧

32

If you reflect on death, there's nothing you
will need;
People of Tingri, always keep your death in
mind.

O nce the conviction that everything is imperma-
nent, the recognition that existence is extremely
fragile, and the awareness that death is an ever-present
threat have truly taken root in your mind, you will
stop hankering after life's ordinary compulsions. You
will wish for nothing more than to be able to practice
the Dharma in a solitary place. Look at Jetsun Milarepa. He had only nettles for sustenance and a cotton
shawl for clothing, yet in a single lifetime he attained
the supreme level of an Awareness Holder. But if you
do not reflect deeply enough on death and impermanence, your lack of perspective will make it difficult to
rid yourself of life's more futile concerns. Your tendency always to want more than you need will con-

tinue. Even though you have enough to eat, you will want ever more delicious food. Despite having enough clothes and an adequate place to live, you will keep thinking about getting something better or more fashionable to wear and a bigger, more comfortable house. Although you may already have a partner or a lover, you will be constantly on the lookout for someone better.

These are all signs that you are not remembering how close death really is, all the time. Why would you invest all that energy on those plans for the future if you were not somehow blindly convinced that you are still sure to be here in this world for a long time to come?

The great practitioners of the past described themselves as "yogis with the thought of impermanence implanted firmly in their hearts." They saw clearly the futility of ordinary pursuits. Their minds were entirely turned toward the Dharma. Their practice of the Dharma was based on a frugal life inspired by the thought of their own death, which they knew would take place in a deserted cave. All these great practitioners, of course, are now dead—for that is the lot of all living beings. But instead of being reborn in the realms of suffering, where all those preoccupied with the pleasures of this life are endlessly caught, they are now in the Buddha-fields.

Such a farsighted and profound perspective can take hold within you. It is the result of being con-

stantly mindful of death. Mindfulness of death is a nec-
tarlike medicine that restores you to health and a
sentinel that watches over the discipline of your practice, never letting it stray into distractions. ❧

33

Like lengthening shadows as the sun sinks
*   low,*
The demon of death relentlessly draws
*   nearer;*
People of Tingri, quickly! Get away from
*   him!*

As the sun sets in the evening, the lengthening
shadows of the western hills draw ever nearer
until they engulf us in the twilight. So, too, do the
shadows of death approach as the sun of our life declines. But there is one important difference—death
does not come at a predictable time and place. From
the very moment of our birth, our lives are ever moving inexorably toward death, but the time of that encounter is anything but certain.

   A hunted criminal never has a tranquil moment.
He is always alert, urgently devising a thousand schemes

to escape the punishment that awaits him. You will never find him drawing plans for his future house.

How can you rest when death threatens to strike at any moment? From now on, your sole recourse must be the practice of Dharma. There is no other way to turn death into something favorable. ❧

34

The morning's ravishing flower will wither
by nightfall;
People of Tingri, don't put your hopes in
your body.

The flowers of all sorts of colors that wave in the summer breezes—will they still be there in the blizzards of winter, or after the hail? The forests turn from green to gold in autumn, and in winter the branches of all the trees stand out dark and lifeless. Our bodies, too, grow older and decline day after day. There is nothing we can do about it. The more you are preoccupied by your own physical aging, the more anxious you will become. Do not worry so much about your physical appearance. Concentrate, rather, on not wasting your life. Practice the Dharma. The more you engage in it, the more your satisfaction will grow. ৯

35

*Even if resembling, while alive, the children
of the gods,
Once dead they are more frightful than a
demon horde;
People of Tingri, you've been deceived by
these illusory bodies.*

Your body may be something of pride to you at the
moment, and you no doubt cherish it and try to
look after it well. Your friends and relatives, too, take
it affectionately by the hand and speak warmly to it,
all smiles. The day after you die, however, everything
will be very different. Your dear ones will do everything they can to get your body out of the door as
quickly as possible. Who wants a corpse in the house?
If you were in Tibet, your body would be bound up
with rope, put in a sack, and carried to the cemetery,
to be dismembered by men and torn to shreds by vultures.

What should you do to put your body to good use? Most people have no idea. A craftsman who borrows some tools will try to make the best possible use of them while they are available. Your body, too, is actually on loan to you for the time being, for the brief period left before it is taken back from you by death. Had you better not use it to practice the Dharma while you can? ❦

36

Visitors to market day, their trading finished,
on the morrow have dispersed;
People of Tingri, your friends will part from
you, be certain.

When a lot of people gather for a party, it is usually a joyous event. They laugh, dance, talk, and enjoy food in the company of numerous friends. But all gatherings, for whatever purpose, eventually come to an end, and everyone present will be dispersed. Once the evening comes, a marketplace that has been swarming with activity all day will be deserted. The members of a united family, happy though they may feel when they are all together, will have to cross the threshold of death one after the other, all alone. ॐ

37

*Since this scarecrow conjured up by magic is
sure to tumble down,
People of Tingri, act now according to the
linking of effect with cause.*

The scarecrow that a farmer puts together and sets
up in his fields to deter birds and wild animals
will probably last only one season. In the wind and
rain, it is soon reduced to rags and tatters. In the same
way, the ephemeral coming together of our body and
mind, which results from the conjunction of various
causes and conditions, will sooner or later disintegrate.

As the time approaches for your body and mind to
finally separate, they will fall prey to the ravages of sickness and old age. You will have neither the time nor the
strength to practice the Dharma, however vividly you
may regret not having practiced earlier. It is now—
now, at this very moment in your life, while you have
all the favorable conditions—that you need to muster

all your energy for practice. The time for traders to display their wares, surely, is it not on market day?

Just planning to study the Dharma will bring you neither knowledge nor wisdom. If you keep postponing any study, reflection, and meditation until later, the time will come when your physical and intellectual faculties will degenerate and you will be unable to engage in any of these things. The spiritual master who could have guided you will leave the world, and you will have wasted your chance.

For the most part, we usually follow after our negative tendencies, which are the result of our past negative actions. Positive tendencies that lead toward Dharma are the rare privilege of those who have devoted themselves to positive actions. As soon as favorable conditions for Dharma practice present themselves, we should apply ourselves strenuously while the opportunity is there—like farmers at harvesttime, who work hard from dawn to dusk, knowing that any delay could mean the loss of their crop.

People apply tremendous effort to accomplish ordinary goals. As the saying goes, "They wear a hat of stars and shoes of frost," because they are still out late at night and start work again at dawn. Should you not put a thousand times more energy into achieving enlightenment, the most important goal of all? ❧

38

For sure, the vulture of your mind will one
day fly away;
People of Tingri, now is the time to soar up
to the heights.

A vulture, when it has finished feeding off a car-
cass, abandons it and soars away. Similarly, when
the time comes, your mind, having finished with this
life, will abandon your corpse and fly off into the
bardo. To go beyond samsara and nirvana, we will need
the two wings of emptiness and compassion. From
now on, let us use these two wings to fly fearlessly into
the sky of the life to come. ॐ

39

All beings of the six realms have cared for
you as parents;
People of Tingri, toward them cultivate
your love and compassion.

Just as space is infinitely vast, so too is the number of sentient beings. Yet we tend to think that the only relationships we have with other beings are the tiny number, comparatively, that we have at present. In our neighborhood, we like a few people, dislike a few others, and ignore all the rest. Based on this prejudiced and very limited perception of others, we keep giving rise to attachment and aggression. Thus we accumulate karma, the driving force of samsara.

If we could see the endless sequence of lives we have led in the past, we would know that there is not a single being on earth who has not been our father or our mother, not only once but many times over. To return the love and great kindness they have shown us, we must cultivate love and compassion for all of them, as the great enlightened ones do. Above all, we should aspire from the depths of our heart to be able to bring them to perfect enlightenment, without leaving a single one of them behind. The merit arising from such an aspiration is in proportion to the number of beings, so the wish to liberate innumerable beings can engender an immeasurable amount of merit.

The foundation for this is a good heart. As Lord Buddha told King Prasanjit, "Great king, your works are vast and numerous. Whether you are seated, whether you march, eat, or are in repose, may all your acts, laws, and judgments be inspired by a good heart. In this way you will confer unlimited benefits on your subjects and accumulate unlimited merit for yourself."

What is meant by a good heart? To look after your present parents lovingly is, of course, proof of a good heart. But your parents are only two people out of all the infinite number of beings. To be truly good-hearted is to see *all* beings—not only friends, but enemies and strangers too—as your parents, and to rid yourself of all hatred, selfishness, and indifference.

Think of the person toward whom you feel the strongest hostility as though he or she were dearest to your heart. If you feel a selfish attachment toward someone close, consider it as an encounter in a dream, a magical illusion devoid of any reality.

Good-heartedness must express itself in tangible benefit to others. But what do you mean by benefit to others? To give food, clothing, shelter, and affection is unquestionably the sign of a good heart, but such kindness is still limited. We should try to help others in a vast, unlimited way, and only the Dharma can enable us to do that.

We should try and help in all sorts of ways, directly and indirectly, in our actions and in our prayers. Pronounce the names of the buddhas and bodhisattvas over an anthill, for example, or a fishpond or aviary, with compassion and the wish "May these myriads of animals be spared rebirth in the lower realms of samsara." There are many such actions that can be of real help. Be inspired by the constant impetus to benefit others, and the *bodhichitta*, the wish to achieve enlightenment for the benefit of all beings, will unfold more and more in you.

Actions cannot be judged by their appearance. Their value depends on our inner attitude. To perform conspicuous acts of charity with a self-centered motive—expecting gratitude, for instance, or a karmic reward—would have nothing to do with good-heartedness. Such motivation deteriorates the qualities of your actions. Keep in mind that the true way of the Mahayana is love and compassion, imbued with the vow to lead all beings to liberation.

Bodhichitta has two aspects, absolute and relative. Absolute bodhichitta is the realization of emptiness, which ripens slowly in the course of time. Relative bodhichitta is an altruism rooted in loving-kindness and compassion, as an attitude and also in action. Cultivated in depth over a long time, the practice of relative bodhichitta will naturally transform your mind until the realization of absolute bodhichitta dawns.

Once a bodhisattva, having fully realized emptiness, becomes a buddha, his compassion no longer works through ordinary conditioned thoughts such as "This being is praying to me for help, I must benefit him" or "That one is not praying." His compassion and the emptiness from which it arises are universal and all-encompassing. Such compassion knows no partiality, attachment, or aversion—in the same way that the sun is reflected equally on any surface of water, whether large or small, clear or muddy. Compassion is the effortless radiance of emptiness, free of concepts and beyond description.

That is how a buddha's activity for beings can be limitless. If you understand this, you will know that even when a cool breeze blows upon a sick person burning with fever, that itself is the blesssings and compassion of the buddhas. ❧

40

Hate for enemies is samsara's hallucination,
caused by actions;
People of Tingri, transmute your hatred and
your hostile mind.

When we suffer a wrong that is inflicted on us without apparent reason, like the wrong done to the Tibetans by the Chinese, it can only be the result of wrongs that we ourselves have inflicted on others in previous lifetimes. It follows that if we respond to violence with more violence, we will only generate more suffering.

If someone steals something valuable from you, do not be upset or depressed, and do not feel anger or regret. Forget about vengeance. In your mind, offer the thief whatever it is he has taken from you and pray that your forbearance serves to purify all your past faults. Love is the only just response to hate.

A story from the Buddha's previous lives shows how patience can be perfected. One day a king out walking in the forest with his court became furious when he discovered that while he had been resting in the shade, his queens had wandered off to sit at the feet of a sage who lived in a nearby clearing. The solitary hermit was Kshantivadin, "Teacher of Patience." Hearing that the sage was supposed to be a master of patience, the king—challenging him in his rage to preserve his famous patience—first severed both Kshantivadin's arms, and then his head. But despite this onslaught the sage truly felt nothing but love and compassion, praying that the king and his queens would become his first disciples when he later became Buddha. ॐ

41

Prostration and circumambulation purify
obscuration of the body;
People of Tingri, abandon all your worldly
physical work.

I f you work from morning until night, plow your
fields, build yourself an imposing house, or travel
around the world, your efforts may bring you financial
rewards and other ephemeral satisfactions. But none
of it will bring you lasting happiness or help you progress on the path to enlightenment.

On the other hand, if you relate all your physical
activities to the Dharma, even a gesture as small as a
simple prostration or circumambulating a temple will
take on a profound significance. The Buddha said that
to offer a single prostration with devotion is sufficient
cause for you to be reborn as a great king, not just once
but as many times as there are grains of dust under

your prostrate body, from the surface of the earth down to the great golden foundation of the universe,[7] and even then your merit will not be exhausted. ❧

42

Recitation and taking refuge purify
obscuration of the speech;
People of Tingri, abandon all your ordinary
conversation.

There is a saying, "The mouth is a box of tricks, the gateway of all faults and all misdeeds." What comes out of peoples' mouths under the influence of negative emotions is chatter, lies, calumny, and harsh words. People seem to have an unlimited appetite for malicious gossip and constant speculation about wars and other bad news, which stir up the emotions even more.

By contrast, simply to utter the words of a prayer, the syllables of a mantra, or the names of the Three Jewels, "Namo Buddhaya, Namo Dharmaya, Namo Sanghaya," can save you from suffering and accomplish great benefits. Whoever hears the names of the buddhas or that of Guru Padmasambhava or the sound of a mantra will be liberated from three great

fears: the fear of the Fundamental Vehicle disciple,
who is terrified of falling into the lower realms of samsara; the fear of the Great Vehicle disciple, who worries about lapsing into egocentric motivation; and the
fear of the Adamantine Vehicle disciple, who dreads
attachment to the reality of phenomena.

As a practitioner of Dharma, in particular, never
indulge in idle chatter. You would do better to have a
prayer always on your lips, or to read aloud the profound texts that explain the relative and absolute aspects of reality. ❧

43

Fervent devotion purifies habitual tendencies
of the mind;
People of Tingri, meditate on the teacher
above your head.

If your mind is constantly preoccupied by your
money and possessions, you are in reality only preparing the ground for rebirth as a spirit tortured by
hunger and thirst. If your thoughts are obsessed with
your family and loved ones, you are only strengthening
the pangs of separation you will suffer when you die.

But to have devotion constantly in your mind will
endow you with lasting serenity and satisfaction. Remembering even the name of your spiritual teacher
is enough to completely transform your perceptions.
Visualizing the guru above the crown of your head,
even for an instant, can dissipate the veils of illusion.
Devotion is the ring that allows the hook of the teacher's compassion to pull you out of the mire of samsara.

Enlightenment, inherent though it is in the mind, seems so difficult to unveil. But if you develop fervent devotion and fuse the guru's enlightened nature with your ordinary mind, enlightenment can be realized. Truly, to meditate on the benevolent teacher is a spiritual practice more profound than any other. ❧

44

Your flesh and bones took form together, but
in the end are sure to separate;
People of Tingri, do not believe that you
will live forever.

In the end, this body made of flesh and bones is destined only to be buried, cremated, thrown into a river, fed to the vultures, or even left to rot. Why be so attached to it? Nevertheless, if you use it to practice the Dharma, your body can indeed be a very precious tool. Before it disintegrates, profit from it by advancing on the path as far as you can. Do not waste its potential in futile enterprises or, even worse, in accumulating harmful actions. ৯৯

45

*Capture that most sublime of countries, the
constant land of the natural state,
People of Tingri, where there is no transition
or change.*

You might buy a piece of land, clear it, build a
house, and cultivate fields, with the idea that
these activities will bring you happiness and satisfaction in the future. But it is simply not so.

The only land really worth claiming is the stronghold of primordial simplicity, the ultimate and unchanging nature of all things. The way to take hold
of it is by solitary meditation, progressing through the
different stages of the path culminating in the Great
Perfection. Once you have taken full possession of it,
you will be able to dwell there for the rest of your life,
after death, and during all your lives to come. But to get
to that point, be ready for a thousand acts of bravery. ❧

46

Enjoy that most sublime of riches, the
treasure of the nature of mind,
People of Tingri, which cannot ever be
depleted.

With enormous effort and determination, you might manage to amass an immense fortune and innumerable possessions. But do you think you can keep hold of those riches forever? However, there are other kinds of wealth—resources such as wisdom, compassion, faith, generosity, and diligence—that multiply as fast as we use them. These precious jewels abound in the very nature of the mind, and are free of all the shortcomings of samsara. ༁

47

Savor that most sublime of foods, the
exquisite taste of meditation,
People of Tingri, which abolishes the pangs
of hunger.

The food you eat might be delicious or insipid, meager or plentiful—but in the end it all turns into excrement. Jetsun Milarepa and other great yogis survived for months without food and without feeling hunger. They knew how to sustain themselves with contemplation and meditation.

Nourish yourself on sustained calm and profound insight, and you will enjoy the savor of serenity in this life and in all your lives to come. You will escape the famine of ignorance and be naturally inclined to meditation. ॐ

48

*Imbibe that most sublime of drinks, the
ambrosia of mindfulness,
People of Tingri, whose flow is never
interrupted.*

Unlike ordinary drinks, the nectar of mindfulness is available everywhere all the time, and can quench your thirst once and for all. Jetsun Milarepa said, "If you need something to drink, drink the tea of mindfulness and vigilance."

If you are gradually going to make your qualities evolve and overcome your faults, you need to be constantly aware of your state of mind, and to be mindful of the importance of your actions and the consequences they may bring. It is essential to maintain mindfulness whatever you are doing, whether you are walking, sitting, eating, or resting. It will give you the strength to face death with confidence. When confronted with the terrifying apparitions of the bardo, you will be able to remember your spiritual teacher and the Three Jewels instantly, which will free you from fear. Vigilance will help you throughout the process of death and rebirth; by availing yourself of the processes of cause and effect, you will continue to progress on the path.

Mindfulness should guide all your actions and your spiritual endeavors. Whatever you do, always apply three essential points: undertake the action with the intention of doing so for the good of all beings; execute it with perfect concentration, free of attachment to concepts of subject, object, and action; and, finally, dedicate the merit you have created to the enlightenment of all beings.

At night, it is good to examine what you have thought and done during the day, and to confess your faults and unconsidered actions and repair them. Tell yourself that, having encountered a teacher and received his instructions, you know better than to behave in that way. As for your positive actions, dedicate the merit to all beings and vow to improve on them the following day. ❧

49

Rely upon that most sublime companion,
   primordial awareness wisdom,
People of Tingri, from which you never can
   be parted.

Sooner or later, you will have to part from even your dearest friends. But one friend will never leave you, even though you may not be aware of its existence. It is the Buddha-nature, pure awareness. You begin to discover it by listening to the teachings of a spiritual master. The ties will deepen as you cultivate sustained mental calm and profound insight into reality. In the end, you will discover that it has always been near you and will always be with you. This is the truest friendship you can ever cultivate. ॐ

50

Seek for that most sublime of progeny, the
young child pure awareness,
People of Tingri, for which there is no birth
or death.

When a child is born, the parents are overjoyed. There is a new addition to their family, the family's continuity is ensured, and when they get old there will be someone to take care of them and their property. However, the powerful attachment to their children that parents experience will often, in the end, bring them more torment than joy. It is particularly difficult for them not to sink into despair when they lose a child before their own time has come.

Moreover, in many instances the parents may have obtained whatever they own through negative actions, and will encourage their children to do the same. In terms of the causes and effects of karma, they actually do each other harm, albeit unwittingly. The parents will be encouraging their children to make use of wealth tarnished by negativity; and the children, by doing so and perpetuating the negativity, will bring harm to their parents.

As your progeny, would it not be better to seek that sublime, innate child, pure awareness? Blinded by delusion, you have lost all sight of him. But if you have the lucidity to find him again, he will stay by your side, and even death will not be able to tear him away. And it is he who will lead you to the stronghold of the nature of mind, the union of pure awareness and emptiness. ❧

51

In a state of emptiness, whirl the spear of
  pure awareness;
People of Tingri, the view is free of being
  caught by anything at all.

Your view should be as high and vast as the sky. Pure awareness, once it manifests within the mind's empty nature, can no longer be obscured by the negative emotions, which become its ornaments instead. The changeless state that is the realization of the view is not something that comes into existence, remains, or ceases; within it, awareness observes the movement of thoughts like a serene old man watching children at play. Confused thoughts cannot affect pure awareness any more than a sword can pierce the sky.

Lady Peldarbum said to Jetsun Milarepa:

When I meditated on the ocean,
My mind was very comfortable.

> When I meditated on the waves,
> My mind was troubled.
> Teach me to meditate on the waves!

The great yogi responded:

> The waves are the movement of the ocean.
> Leave them to subside by themselves in its
>   vastness.

Thoughts are the play of pure awareness. They arise within it and dissolve back into it. To recognize pure awareness as where your thoughts come from is to recognize that your thoughts have never come into existence, remained, or ceased. At that point, thoughts can no longer trouble your mind.

When you run after your thoughts, you are like a dog chasing a stick: every time a stick is thrown, you run after it. But if, instead, you look at where your thoughts are coming from, you will see that each thought arises and dissolves within the space of that awareness, without engendering other thoughts. Be like a lion—who, rather than chasing after the stick, turns to face the thrower. One only throws a stick at a lion once.

To take the uncreated stronghold of the nature of mind, you have to go to the source and recognize the very origin of your thoughts. Otherwise, one thought will give rise to a second, then a third, and so on. In no time, you will be assailed by memories of the past and anticipation of the future, and the pure awareness of the present moment will be completely obscured.

There is a story about a practitioner who was feeding the pigeons outside with the rice he had offered on his altar, when he suddenly remembered the numerous enemies he had had before devoting himself to the Dharma. The thought came to him, "There are so many pigeons at my door now; if I had had that many soldiers then, I could easily have wiped out my enemies."

This idea obsessed him until he could no longer control his hostility, and he left his hermitage, assembled a band of mercenaries, and went to fight his former enemies. The negative actions he then committed all began with that one simple, deluded thought.

If you recognize the emptiness of your thoughts instead of solidifying them, the arising and subsiding of each thought will clarify and strengthen your realization of emptiness. ❧

52

In a state without thoughts, without
distraction abandon the watcher;
People of Tingri, the meditation is free of
any torpor or excitement.

When your mind remains in pure awareness, with no thought of past or future, without being attracted by external objects or occupied by mental constructions, it will be in a state of primordial simplicity. In that state, there is no need for the iron hand of forced vigilance to immobilize your thoughts. As it is said, "Buddhahood is the natural simplicity of the mind."

Once you have recognized that simplicity, you need to maintain that recognition with effortless presence of mind. Then you will experience an inner freedom in which there is no need to block the arising of thoughts, or fear that they will spoil your meditation. ༃

53

In a state of natural spontaneity, train in
being free of any holding back;
People of Tingri, in the action there is
nothing to abandon or adopt.

Preserve that state of simplicity. Should you encounter happiness, success, and other favorable
conditions, take them like a dream or an illusion. Do
not get attached to them. And should you be struck by
illness, calumny, or other trials, physical or mental, do
not let yourself be discouraged. Rekindle your compassion by wishing that through your own suffering, the
sufferings of all beings might be exhausted. Whatever
the circumstances, do not get either elated or depressed, but remain free and at ease in imperturbable
serenity. ༀ

54

*The four bodies, indivisible, are complete in
your mind;
People of Tingri, the fruit is beyond all hope
and doubt.*

Buddhahood may seem far away, a distant goal almost beyond reach, but in truth the emptiness that is the essential nature of your mind is nothing other than the "absolute body," or dharmakaya. The clarity that is its natural expression is the "body of perfect endowment," or sambhogakaya. The all-pervading compassion that emanates from it is the "body of manifestation," or nirmanakaya. The intrinsic oneness of these three bodies is the "body of the nature as it is," or svabhavikakaya. These four bodies, or dimensions, of a buddha have always been present within you. It is only because you do not know that they are there that you think of them as being somewhere outside and far away.

"Is my meditation correct?" you wonder, restlessly. "When am I finally going to make some progress? I'll never attain the level of my spiritual master." Torn between hope and fear, your mind is never at peace.

According to your mood, you practice intensely one day and the next day not at all. You cling to the agreeable experiences that arise when you attain sustained mental calm, but feel like abandoning the meditation when you cannot slow down the flood of thoughts. That is not the way to practice meditation.

Whatever state of mind you find yourself in, keep up a regular practice, day after day, observing the movement of your thoughts and following them back to their source. You cannot expect to be able to maintain the flow of your concentration day and night from the very start.

When you start meditating on the nature of the mind, it is preferable to practice in short, frequent sessions. With perseverance, you will progressively recognize and realize the nature of your mind, and this realization will become more and more stable. By that point, thoughts will have lost their power to disturb and enslave you. ❧

55

The root of both samsara and nirvana is to
be found within your mind;
People of Tingri, the mind is free of any true
reality.

It is our own minds that lead us astray into the cycle of existence. Blind to the mind's true nature, we fixate on our thoughts, which in truth are simply the manifestations of that nature. But through fixation, pure awareness is frozen into solid concepts such as "self" and "other," "desirable" and "repulsive," and many more. That is how we create samsara.

If we can melt the ice of these fixations by following a teacher's instructions, pure awareness recovers its natural fluidity. To put it another way, if you cut through a tree at the base of the trunk, the trunk, branches, and leaves all fall together. Similarly, if you cut through thoughts at their source, the whole delusion of samsara will collapse.

Everything we experience—all the phenomena of samsara and nirvana—appears with the vivid clarity of a rainbow and yet, like a rainbow, is devoid of any tangible reality. Once you recognize the nature of phenomena—manifest and at the same time empty—your mind will be freed from the tyranny of delusion.

To recognize the ultimate nature of the mind is to realize the state of Buddhahood, and to fail to recognize it is to sink into ignorance. In either case, it is your mind, and your mind alone, that liberates or binds you.

That does not mean, however, that the mind is an entity to be worked on, like a piece of clay that a potter can change into any shape. When the teacher introduces the disciple to the nature of the mind, he is not pointing to some concrete object. When the disciple seeks and finds that nature, he does not take hold of some entity that can be grasped. To recognize the nature of the mind is to recognize its emptiness. That is all. It is a realization that takes place in the realm of direct experience, and cannot be expressed in words.

To expect such a realization to be accompanied by clairvoyance, miraculous powers, and other extraordinary experiences would be to delude yourself. Just devote yourself to recognizing the empty nature of the mind! ❧

56

Desire and hate appear, but like birds in
flight should leave no trace behind;
People of Tingri, in meditation be free of
clinging to experiences.

Generally speaking, we feel attachment to our family, to our belongings, and to our position, and aversion to anyone who hurts or threatens us. Try turning your attention away from such external objects and examine the mind that identifies them as desirable or hateful. Do your desire and anger have any form, color, substance, or location? If not, why is it that you fall so easily under the power of such feelings?

It is because you do not know how to set them free. If you allow your thoughts and feelings to arise and dissolve by themselves, they will pass through your mind in the same way as a bird flies through the sky, without leaving any trace. This applies not only to attachment and anger, but also to the experiences of meditation—bliss, clarity, and the absence of thought. These experiences result from perseverance in practice and are the expression of the inherent creativity of the mind. They appear like a rainbow, formed as the rays of the sun strike a curtain of rain; and to become attached to them is as futile as it would be to run after a rainbow in the hopes of wearing it as a coat. Simply allow your thoughts and experiences to come and go, without ever grasping at them. ❧

57

The unborn absolute body is like the very
heart of the sun—
People of Tingri, there is no waxing or
waning of its radiant clarity.

The dharmakaya, the absolute dimension, the ultimate nature of everything, is emptiness. But it is
not mere nothingness. It has a cognitive, radiant clarity
aspect that knows all phenomena and manifests spon-
taneously. The dharmakaya is not something produced
by causes and conditions; it is the primordially present
nature of the mind.

The recognition of this primordial nature is like
the sun of wisdom rising and piercing through the
night of ignorance. The darkness is dissipated instantly; the shadows cannot remain. The clarity of the
dharmakaya does not wax and wane like the moon,
but is like the unchangeable brilliance that reigns at
the center of the sun. ☙

58

Thoughts come and go like a thief in an
empty house—
People of Tingri, in fact there is nothing to
be gained or lost.

Convinced of the reality of an entity called "I" and its thoughts, we follow after those thoughts and feelings and act upon them, creating karmic results, good or bad. In reality, thoughts are like a thief in an empty house, where the thief has nothing to gain and the owner has nothing to lose. To realize that thoughts never really come into existence, and can therefore neither remain nor cease to exist, is enough to render them harmless. Thoughts liberated in this way as they arise have no impact and bring no karmic effect. There will be nothing to fear from negative thoughts, and nothing to hope for from positive ones. ॐ

59

Sensations leave no imprints, like drawings
made on water;
People of Tingri, don't perpetuate deluded
appearances.

We are naturally attached to comfort and pleasure and bothered by physical and mental suffering. These innate tendencies lead us to seek out,
maintain, and try to increase whatever gives us pleasure—comfortable clothing, delicious food, agreeable
places, sensual pleasure—and to avoid or destroy whatever we find unpleasant or painful.

Constantly changing and devoid of any true essence,
these sensations rest on the ephemeral association of the
mind with the body, and it is useless to be attached to
them. Rather than being dragged along and trapped by
your perceptions, just let them dissolve as soon as they
form, like letters traced on the surface of water with your
finger that disappear as you draw them. ❧

60

Thoughts of attachment and aversion are
like rainbows in the sky;
People of Tingri, there is nothing in them to
be grasped or apprehended.

People can be so dominated by their craving or
their hatred that they are even willing to lose their
lives to satisfy it, as wars so tragically illustrate. Your
own thoughts and feelings of attachment and aversion
may seem very solid and compelling, but if you examine them carefully you will see that they have no more
substance than a rainbow. To devote your life to trying
to satisfy such impulses, to hunger for power, pleasures, and riches, would surely be as puerile as a child
wanting to catch a rainbow.

In practice, whenever a strong desire or a burst of
anger inflames your mind, look closely at your thoughts
and recognize their fundamental emptiness. If you
allow them to, those thoughts and feelings will dissolve

by themselves. When you can do the same with the next thought and with all that follow, they will lose their hold over you. ❧

61

Mind's movements dissolve by themselves,
like clouds in the sky;
People of Tingri, in the mind there are no
reference points.

When banks of clouds gather in the sky, the nature of the sky is not impaired. Nor, when they disperse, is it improved. The sky is made neither more vast or pure, nor less so. It is not changed or affected at all. The nature of the mind is just the same. It is not altered by the arising of thoughts, nor by their disappearance.

The essential nature of the mind is emptiness. Its natural expression is clarity. These two aspects of the mind can be distinguished for descriptive purposes, but they are essentially one. Fixating on the notion of emptiness or of clarity alone as if these were independent entities is a mistake. The ultimate nature of the mind is beyond all concepts, definitions, and partial views.

A child might think, "I could walk on those clouds!" If he actually found himself in the clouds, however, he would find nowhere to set foot. In the same way, your thoughts appear to be solid until you examine them. Then you find that they are without any substance. This is what we call the simultaneous appearance and emptiness of things. ❧

62

Without fixation, thoughts are freed by
themselves—like the wind,
People of Tingri, which never clings to any
object.

The wind blows through the sky and flies across continents without ever settling anywhere. It sweeps through space, leaving no trace whatsoever. Let thoughts pass through your mind in the same way, leaving no karmic residue and never altering your realization of innate simplicity. ॐ

63

*Pure awareness is without fixation, like a
  rainbow in the sky;
People of Tingri, experiences arise quite
  unimpededly.*

P ure awareness, the enlightened mind, which is
   simply the mind liberated of all delusion, transcends the very notions of existing or not existing.

"Where there is attachment, there is no view"
were the words that the great Sakya master Jetsun
Trakpa Gyaltsen heard from Manjushri, the Buddha
of Wisdom, during a vision. Enlightenment cannot be
said to exist, because even the buddhas have not seen
it. Nor can it be said not to exist, because it is the
source of samsara and nirvana. As long as concepts
such as existing and not existing persist, you have not
realized the mind's true nature.

A rainbow gleaming in the sky, although it could
be called a manifestation of the sky, is really nothing

other than the sky itself. Similarly, the experiences that arise in your mind when you meditate—the good experiences that lead you to believe you have attained realization, and the bad ones that discourage you—in fact have no substantial existence of their own. The saying goes, "Meditators taken in by their experiences are like children lured by a rainbow." Lend no importance to such experiences, and they will never be able to lead you astray. ❧

64

Realization of the absolute nature is like the
dream of a mute;
People of Tingri, there are no words to
express it.

For someone without the faculty of speech, a beautiful dream, clearly remembered though it might be, is impossible to describe in words. In the same way, the nature of the mind is beyond any description; no words can define its ultimate nature, the dharmakaya. You could say it exists, but there is nothing you can show of it but emptiness. Or you could say it is nothing at all, but then how do you explain its myriad manifestations? The ultimate nature of the mind defies all description and cannot be grasped by discursive thought. ॐ

65

Realization is like a youthful maiden's
pleasure;
People of Tingri, the joy and bliss just
cannot be described.

With the dawn of realization, the mind becomes perfectly free, at ease, fulfilled, vast, and serene. This realization, however, is inexpressible, like the joy of an adolescent in the flower of youth. ॐ

66

Clarity and emptiness united are like the
moon reflected in water;
People of Tingri, there is nothing to be
attached to and nothing to impede.

Everything we perceive, all phenomena throughout samsara and nirvana, arises simply as the play
of the mind's natural creativity. This "clarity" of the
mind—the distinct appearance of phenomena to our
perception—is the radiance of the mind's empty nature. Emptiness is the very essence of clarity, and clarity is the expression of emptiness. They are indivisible.

The mind, like a reflection of the moon in the still
surface of a lake, is brilliantly apparent, but you cannot
take hold of it. It is vividly present and at the same
time utterly intangible. By its very nature, which is the
indivisible union of emptiness and clarity, nothing can
obstruct it and it can obstruct nothing, unlike a solid

object, such as a rock, with a physical presence occupying space and excluding other objects. In essence, the mind is insubstantial and omnipresent. ❧

67

Appearances and emptiness inseparable are
*   like the empty sky;*
People of Tingri, the mind is without either
*   center or periphery.*

The mind apprehends forms, sounds, and other phenomena, and experiences happiness and suffering. Yet the world of appearances has never existed in itself. When you analyze it, there is only emptiness. Just as physical empty space provides the dimensions in which whole worlds can unfold, so too does the empty nature of the mind provide the space for its own expressions to appear. And just as physical space is limitless, with no center or periphery, so too the mind is without beginning or end, in both space and time. ॐ

68

*The mind with no thought and no
    distraction is like the mirror of a
    beauty;
People of Tingri, it is free of any theoretical
    tenets.*

Once you have recognized the nature of the mind, you no longer need to restrict yourself to a conscious recollection of that nature, or to modify it in any way. At that point, the mind cannot even be said to be in "meditation," because it naturally stays at rest in a state of serene integration. There is no need to concentrate on the details of a particular visualization, such as the form of a deity. The mind will not stray into the distraction and delusion that characterize the ordinary state, because it stays continually and effortlessly in its own nature.

Awareness is not affected by agreeable or disagreeable perceptions. It simply stays as it is, in the same way that a mirror when it reflects people's faces is neither enraptured by their beauty nor offended by their ugliness. And just as a mirror reflects all forms faithfully and with absolute impartiality, so too an enlightened being clearly perceives all phenomena without his realization of the ultimate nature being affected in any way.

An image reflected in a mirror is neither part of the mirror nor is it elsewhere than in the mirror. In the same way, the phenomena we perceive are neither in the mind nor outside it. Indeed, a true realization of the ultimate nature of things goes utterly beyond any concepts of being or nonbeing. Thus Nagarjuna said in *The Root Stanzas of the Middle Way:* "Since I affirm nothing, no one can refute my point of view." ≋

69

*Awareness and emptiness inseparable are
    like reflections in a mirror;
People of Tingri, nothing is born there and
    nothing ceases.*

The empty nature of the mind is not a state of
blank torpor or mere nothingness. Rather, it has
the faculty of knowing, a naturally present clarity that
we call awareness or enlightened consciousness. These
two aspects of the mind's nature, emptiness and awareness, are essentially one, like a mirror and the reflection
in it.

Thoughts take form within emptiness and dissolve
there, as the reflection of a face appears and disappears
in a mirror. Since the reflection of the face never was
actually in the mirror, it does not cease to be when it
is no longer reflected there.

Nor does the mirror itself ever change. Before you
start out on the spiritual path, you are in the suppos-

edly impure state of samsara, which, in relative terms, is governed by ignorance. Once you engage in the path, the different states you go through are a mixture of ignorance and knowledge. At the end of the path, at the moment of awakening, nothing remains but awareness. Throughout all the stages of the path, although it might look as if some transformation is taking place, the nature of the mind itself never changes. It is not corrupted at the beginning of the path; it is not improved at the end. ❧

70

*Bliss and emptiness inseparable are like the
sun lighting up the snows;
People of Tingri, there is nothing there to
apprehend.*

When the sun's rays strike the snows of a mountain peak, their whiteness becomes even more
dazzling. But can you distinguish the brilliance of the
sunlight from the whiteness of the snow?

When you recognize the mind's emptiness, the
bliss inherent in it is amplified. It is the bliss of perfect
freedom, at ease and naturally unhindered. However,
it should never be taken as something real to hold on
to. Bliss and emptiness are inseparable. Dazzling
though it is, the brilliance of the snow is not something
you can hold in your hands. ॐ

71

Deluded talk will fade without a trace, like
echoes;
People of Tingri, in sound there is nothing
to be grasped.

We like to hear compliments. If someone praises you, you want them to say more and the whole world to hear. On the other hand, faced with criticism or malicious rumors, you would move heaven and earth to prevent those words from being heard and spreading far and wide.

In reality, however, praise and blame are only empty sounds, unworthy of the slightest attention. It is as ridiculous to be troubled by them as it would be to swell with pride, or take offence, at the echoes sent back by a cliff. ৡ

72

Happiness and suffering, through a
*   mechanism like the sounding of a lute's*
*   body and strings,*
People of Tingri, are produced when actions
*   are combined with necessary*
*   conditions.*

A fine piece of wood is shaped into the form of a
lute, and the strings are set so that a melodious
sound can be drawn from the instrument. Should any
of the necessary elements be lacking, the lute cannot
produce music. In the same way, you cannot expect to
enjoy happiness without having correctly assembled
the basis from which it can arise. Happiness and suffering result from the complex interaction of our positive and negative actions.

Just as mastering the art of the lute requires assidu-
ous practice, mastery of happiness demands the contin-
uous practice of Dharma—and skillful practice at that.

Approaching the Dharma with an undisciplined thirst for gratification will work no better than fervent attempts to make music by the clumsy random plucking of a musical instrument's strings.

From an absolute viewpoint, joy and suffering have no substantial reality whatsoever. They nevertheless depend, on a relative level, on the inexorable laws of cause and effect, just as music follows the laws of harmony.

To use another image, just as there are mushrooms that look and taste delicious but are mortally poisonous to anyone imprudent enough to eat them, so, too, wealth, fame, and sensual pleasures, which seem very attractive at the outset, will end in bitter disappointment. Conversely, just as a medicine that has a very bitter taste may nevertheless be the effective cure for sickness, so too spiritual practice—despite the difficulties and ordeals, both physical and mental, it may entail—leads nevertheless to an indestructible bliss beyond all trace of suffering.

It is thus vital to distinguish what you should adopt from what you should reject, without any error or ambiguity. ❧

73

*The natural freedom of samsara and nirvana
is like a children's game;
People of Tingri, have a mind without any
aims.*

Our endless wandering in samsara is the result of our negative emotions. But take the trouble to examine the nature of these emotions with which we are so obsessed and which are the very cause of the round of existence, and you will find that they do not have the least trace of reality. You will discover nothing but emptiness.

True nirvana comprises the infinite, inexpressible qualities of primordial wisdom. These qualities are innate in the mind; there is no need to invent or create them. Realization uncovers them in the course of the path. Even these qualities, from an ultimate point of view, are simply emptiness.

Both samsara and nirvana are thus emptiness. It follows that neither one of them can be said to be bad or good. When you realize the nature of the mind, you are liberated from the need to reject samsara and pursue nirvana. Seeing the world with all the unspoiled simplicity of a young child, you are free from concepts of beauty and ugliness, good and evil, and no longer fall prey to conflicting tendencies driven by desire or repulsion.

Why trouble yourself about all the ups and downs of daily life, like a child who delights in building a sand castle but cries when it collapses? To get what they want and be rid of what they dislike, look how people throw themselves into torments, like moths plunging into the flame of a lamp! Would it not be better to put down your heavy burden of dreamlike obsessions once and for all? ॐ

74

*Your notions of the outer world derive from
the mind within;
People of Tingri, let the solid ice be melted
into liquid.*

Lakes and rivers can freeze in winter and the water can become so solid that people, animals, and carts travel back and forth on its surface. At the approach of spring, the earth warms up and the waters thaw. What remains then of all that solid ice? Water is soft and fluid, ice hard and sharp. We cannot say that they are identical, but neither are they different—ice is only frozen water, and water is only melted ice.

It is the same with our perceptions of the external world. To be attached to the reality of phenomena, tormented by attraction and repulsion, and obsessed by the eight worldly preoccupations[8] is what causes the mind to freeze. Melt the ice of your concepts so that the fluid water of free perception can flow. ❧

75

The mechanism of ignorance is like the gush
of a meadow spring;
People of Tingri, it cannot be halted by
obstructing it.

During innumerable lifetimes you have main-
tained a stubborn belief in the true existence of
both yourself as an individual and of phenomena as a
whole. The hold that this belief has on you is too
strong for you to be able to free yourself from it simply
by denying that these entities really exist. What is
needed is for you to recognize clearly and directly for
yourself that neither the "I" nor phenomena have any
reality whatsoever.

If you tried to stem the flow of water from a spring
by blocking it with your hand or damming it with a
stone, the pressure of the water would overpower your
efforts in a few seconds. Similarly, any attempt to block
the strong flow of thoughts that often arises during

meditation will probably fail, and could even bring the risk of mental problems. Thoughts and feelings that you have tried to suppress will reemerge as enemies to your meditation.

The right approach is to recognize that your thoughts never really come into existence to begin with, and can thus neither remain in existence nor cease to be. No matter how numerous they might be, if you know how to liberate them at the moment they arise, they will cause you no harm. Your meditation will neither be spoiled by thoughts, nor improved by their absence.

The towns and countryside that the traveler sees through a train window do not slow down the train, nor does the train affect them. Neither disturbs the other. This is how you should see the thoughts that pass through your mind when you meditate. ❧

76

*The delusions of samsara and nirvana are
like coming face to face with an enemy;
People of Tingri, as your ally practice virtue.*

You may have the idea that samsara is something that you must reject at all costs, and that nirvana is something you must strive hard to attain. But such dualistic notions are actually mistaken. They are the fruit of delusion, which in turn is based on ignorance.

Neutralizing delusion is like capturing the general of an opposing army, which will then quickly surrender. To capture the general, however, you need allies—the spiritual teacher and virtuous actions. It is only with their help that you will be able to purify and develop the potential for enlightenment, which in fact is already innate within you. ॐ

77

*The natural clarity of the five kayas is like
the expanse of a continent of gold;
People of Tingri, have no hope or doubt,
attachment, or aversion.*

The state of Buddhahood comprises five "bodies" (*kayas*), or aspects of enlightenment: the body of manifestation, the body of perfect endowment, the absolute body, the body of the nature as it is, and the immutable adamantine body.[9] It is no good looking for them outside of yourself, for they are inseparable from ordinary mind. As soon as you can acknowledge their presence, delusion will vanish, and there will be no need to seek enlightenment elsewhere. An explorer landing on an island made entirely of gold will find no ordinary stones, even if he goes looking for them. You have to discover that the qualities of Buddhahood have always been inherently present within yourself.

It is useless to worry about the slowness of your progress and to get discouraged, thinking that enlightenment is beyond your reach and will happen only in the distant future. Such an attitude will reinforce your anxiety and undermine your ability to practice with a calm mind. As Jetsun Milarepa said, "Do not be impatient to attain enlightenment, but practice until your last breath."

Banishing all hope and all fear, rest in the diamond-like certainty that the primordial simplicity of awareness is itself Buddhahood. That is the way of perfect bliss, in which all the qualities of enlightenment will flourish without effort. ॐ

78

*With its freedoms and advantages, human
life is like a treasure island;
People of Tingri, do not come back an
empty-handed failure.*

An explorer who discovers a treasure island can fill
his ship with gold, diamonds, sapphires, rubies,
and emeralds. But his good fortune has nothing to com-
pare with human life, which offers us something far
more precious than any gold and precious stones—the
chance to reflect on and practice the Dharma and give
meaning to our lives. The treasures we have to choose
from are the various teachings offered by the Fundamental, the Great, and the Adamantine Vehicles.

It is now, while you enjoy all the favorable conditions
of human life, that you have the freedom necessary to
practice the Dharma.[10] To ignore such an opportunity
would be like a beggar picking up a jewel and, taking it
for a piece of glass, tossing it back in the dust. Worse still

would be actually to comprehend the value of human life but to waste it knowingly in distraction and the pursuit of worldly ambitions. That is the epitome of delusion. The explorer who returned from that treasure island empty-handed would have crossed the seas in vain. Do not make such a mistake. ❧

79

The practice of the Great Vehicle is like a
wish-fulfilling gem;
People of Tingri, however hard you search,
it will be difficult to find again.

The miraculous stone called the wish-fulfilling gem has the power to grant all desires and aspirations, and can dispel the misery of an entire country. It is a fitting analogy for the Great Vehicle, which has the power to assuage the suffering of all beings.

In this present life, you have encountered a spiritual teacher and received teachings on the practice of the Great Vehicle. Such an encounter is not due to chance, but results from an inclination toward the spiritual life developed through many past lives.

A qualified spiritual teacher and his teachings are as rare and precious as the blue lotus known as Udumvara, whose buds form when a buddha appears in the world, open when he attains enlightenment, and wither when he leaves his body.

The Buddha has manifested in our world; he has turned the wheel of the teachings, and these teachings have survived until now. You have received them from an authentic teacher and are ready to put them into practice. Rather than frittering your life away in futile pursuits, should you not marvel at your good fortune and concentrate all your efforts on doing just that, without losing so much as an instant? ❧

80

For this life, come what may, you'll have
enough to eat and clothe yourself;
People of Tingri, put everything you have
into practicing the Dharma.

Even if your storerooms and wardrobes are full,
you can still only eat one meal and wear one garment at a time. In truth, all you need is enough nourishment to keep going and clothing to protect you
from the elements. As for these two necessities, do not
worry about them: the Buddha promised that no one
will ever find the bones of a renunciate who has died
of hunger or cold. What is the use of hesitating out of
concern that you will not have enough to eat, nothing
to put on your back, and nowhere to sleep? The
Dharma is the best way of using your life—have no
doubt about it. ॐ

81

*While you are young, practice hard and with
     austerities;
People of Tingri, once you're old your
     constitution won't withstand it.*

It is when you are young that you should take advantage of your youth to practice the Dharma. That is the time when the intellectual faculties required for studying, reflecting, and meditating are at their peak, and when you have the physical strength to endure the rigors of spiritual training. If you can practice to the utmost at that time, later when you are older your practice will have acquired sufficient stability to continue to flourish without effort.

If you put things off and let time pass, your vision will weaken, you will become hard of hearing, you will lose your memory, get tired, and fall ill. It will be too late to begin to practice Dharma. Make the best use of your youth, and have no regrets when you get old. ༀ

82

When emotions arise, bring antidotes to bear
on them;
People of Tingri, let free all concepts in their
very nature.

A merchant crossing a forest infested with thieves would keep a weapon ready to hand. A traveler passing through a country ravaged by plague would take with him an assortment of medicines. In the same way, living as you do under the constant threat of emotions like anger, desire, pride, jealousy, and many others, you should always be ready to fight them off with the appropriate antidotes. Constant vigilance is the mark of a sincere practitioner. You may know how to practice when everything is going well, but that is of little use if you succumb to the first emotion that hits you.

Good practitioners can be recognized by their response to difficult situations liable to provoke latent emotions. Those capable of reacting immediately with the correct antidote will have no problem overcoming obstacles.

In particular, if they know how to transcend the concepts of subject and object, all their thoughts will liberate themselves, like a snake wriggling out of the knots tied in its own body, without effort or help. When you trace all thoughts and concepts back to their very source, you will recognize that they all have the same true nature—emptiness inseparable from transcendent wisdom. ❧

83

Think from time to time of all the defects of
samsara;
People of Tingri, that will make your faith
become much clearer.

There are bound to be troubled times when your diligence fails, your desires are inflamed, and dissatisfaction makes you wish things were different from how they actually are. At such times when you cannot concentrate on practice, reflect on the misery of samsara. To remind yourself clearly that the cycle of existence is entirely permeated by suffering will revive your faith and reaffirm your confidence in the teachings. ૐ

84

Right now, develop diligence and stand your ground;
People of Tingri, when you die it will guide you on the path.

The leader of a powerful army, well-stocked with ammunition, keeps his composure when seeing the enemy advance. Similarly, the meditator who attains unshakable stability in his practice stays calm in the face of death. Now is the time to develop such stability.

A wise traveler prepares for his departure by assembling everything he will need: provisions, money, medicines, maps, and a compass. Sooner or later you will have to set out on the long journey of your future lives, so you had better prepare for it now by taking counsel from a teacher and putting his instructions carefully into practice. ❀

85

*If you're not free now, when will you ever
get to be free?
People of Tingri, your chance to eat comes
only one time in a hundred.*

People often say, "I would love to practice the Dharma,
but for the moment it's impossible. First I must take
care of my family and provide for their future."

But it is now, while you still have a human life, that
you have the opportunity, the freedom and the motivation to follow the Dharma. Why put it off? Are you so
sure you will find better conditions in lives to come? By
then you may be completely caught in suffering and
servitude in the lower realms. If you allow the months
and years to slip by, the opportunity to free yourself
from the vicious circle of samsara will be wasted.

When a delicious feast is offered to you, take it
while you can. The clock of Dharma has struck noon—
seize the chance before it passes! ॐ

86

Life is so ephemeral, like the dew on the
grass;
People of Tingri, don't yield to laziness and
indifference.

Life is fragile, like a dewdrop poised on the tip of a blade of grass, ready to be carried away by the first breath of morning breeze. It is not enough just to have a sincere desire to practice the Dharma and the intention to begin soon. Do not just passively wait for the wind of death to carry away your plans before you have gotten around to them. As soon as the idea of practicing comes to you, do it without hesitation.

Novice practitioners have changeable minds, vulnerable to the emotions, like long grass on a mountain pass bending with the prevailing wind. ৶

87

From where you are now, should you lose
your footing,
People of Tingri, it will be hard to find a
human life again.

I f a mountaineer skirting the slippery rock at the edge of a precipice makes a single false step, it can cost him his life. But throughout your entire human life you have been edging alongside the abyss of the lower realms, running far greater risks than any mountaineer. Once you fall, it is virtually impossible to climb back up the slope that leads to the good fortune of the human realm. The practice of the Dharma is the only thing that will allow you to traverse it safely. ঌ

88

*The Buddha's teaching is like the sun
    shining through clouds;
People of Tingri, now is the one time it is
    present.*

The teachings of the Buddha are not eternally available. When the merit of all the beings living in a particular time period declines, the teachings also decline. Indeed, we are now living at the edge of just such a dark age, the "age of the five degenerations,"[11] in which the setting sun of Dharma is about to sink behind the western mountains. From time to time, nevertheless, it can still shine forth, like the evening sun when there is a gap between the clouds—and those fleeting moments are the only chance we will get. Once night has fallen, an era of darkness will begin in which not even the name of the Three Jewels will be heard.

To take up and follow the teachings is therefore not something that can wait until you feel you are

ready. If you are still wandering in the maze of samsara, it is because in your past lives you either never
encountered the Buddha's teachings, or ignored them.
But now, if you manage to set out on the path, the
good fortune of so doing will sustain you as you progress from excellence to excellence. ❧

89

You say such clever things to people, but
don't apply them to yourself;
People of Tingri, the faults within you are
the ones to be exposed.

There are people who can speak eloquently about the Dharma without having had any true, personal experience of it. But even as their fine words overflow, the fire of the five poisons is all the time burning inside them. Anyone who is going to truly teach others must first have a thorough grounding in the teachings. The steady flame of a stout wick can light a hundred butter lamps, but the tenuous flame of a wick that is too thin cannot even keep itself alight.

You may have received numerous instructions and know, in theory, how to progress and avoid obstacles. Nevertheless, if you do not apply these instructions to yourself, your knowledge will remain sterile, like the wealth of a rich miser who deprives himself of food and starves to death.

If you sincerely want to progress, open your eyes to your own defects. It is your own mind that you must examine, as if in a mirror. To maintain a conceited opinion of yourself, seeing defects only in others and regarding your own flaws as good qualities, will certainly prevent you from making any progress. According to the Kadampa masters, the best teachings expose our hidden faults. To unmask a hitherto unsuspected thief effectively puts an end to his doings.

Know how to recognize your predominant defects, the five poisons—desire, hatred, jealousy, pride, and ignorance. Remain aware of them and be ready to neutralize them whenever they appear. Keep track of your emotions, like a king who fears his enemies and surrounds himself day and night with vigilant guards. The Kadampa masters used to say:

> I hold the sword of vigilance at the gate of
>   my mind.
> When the emotions threaten, I threaten
>   them back.
> Only when they relax their grip,
> Do I relax mine.

To thus maintain constant vigilance, even when under the sway of your emotions, is essential. If you are not even aware of your own emotions, it will be all too easy to miss the point while deluding yourself into thinking that you are really following the Dharma. This kind of mistaken practice can lead to the lower realms.

Just looking at a beautiful fresco depicting all the details of the celestial realms is not the same as actually reaching them. Just reading the doctor's prescription will not make you well. Just imitating the behavior of a Dharma practitioner will not lead you to liberation. To dye a piece of cloth carelessly is a waste of time— the dye will not remain, and nothing will have been accomplished. It is just as pointless to practice the Dharma without it penetrating your being. You will only be squandering your potential. No one can travel the path for you. You must do it yourself. Of course you will not be able to eliminate all your faults at once. Only a buddha is perfect. But you can purify yourself little by little, like the moon emerging resplendent from a sea of clouds.

No crime is so grave that it cannot be repaired. The serial killer Angulimala committed 999 murders, but he became an *arhat* after meeting the Buddha and purifying his misdeeds through the strength of his faith. Any quality can be developed with enough effort. But without having faith or making an effort, you will never perfect yourself, not even if the Buddha himself were to appear to you in person.

Your first thought in the morning should be to dedicate the coming day to the happiness of all beings. Throughout the day, put the teachings into practice. In the evening examine what you have done, said, and thought during the day. Whatever was positive, dedicate the merit to all beings and vow to improve on it the next day. Whatever was negative, confess and promise to repair it. In this way, the best of practitioners progresses from day to day, the middling practitioner from month to month, and the least capable from year to year. ❦

90

That faith succumbs to circumstance is only
a short step away;
People of Tingri, contemplate samsara's
imperfections.

I n the presence of spiritual teachers, listening to their
teachings, you may find it relatively easy to feel
faith and confidence. But the mind is fickle, and your
newborn faith is fragile and can easily succumb to the
changing circumstances of samsara. When your faith
falters, your practice will stagnate.

Faith, therefore, needs nourishing, and the best
way to nourish and revive it is to contemplate the compassion and goodness of the teachers and the Dharma,
comparing that perfection with the unsatisfactory nature of samsara. If you pooled all the tears you have
shed in your past lives, they would form a vast ocean.
If you piled up all the bodies you have had—even just
the bodies from rebirths as insects—the heap would

rise higher than the highest mountain. With the help of such images, contemplate the sheer blindness of your compulsion to plunge into samsara, and try instead to see samsara as a terrible prison from which you must try to break free. ॐ

91

Frequenting evil friends is bound to make
your own behavior evil;
People of Tingri, abandon any friendships
that are negative.

Mind, like a crystal, is colored by its surroundings. You are bound to reflect the qualities and short-comings of the good or bad friends whose company you keep. If you associate with the malevolent, the selfish, the rancorous, the intolerant, and the arrogant, their faults will affect you. You would do better to keep your distance. ॐ

92

*Frequenting virtuous friends is bound to
make your own good qualities arise;
People of Tingri, follow your spiritual
teachers.*

It is always beneficial to be near a spiritual teacher. These masters are like gardens of medicinal plants, sanctuaries of wisdom. In the presence of a realized master, you will rapidly attain enlightenment. In the presence of an erudite scholar, you will acquire great knowledge. In the presence of a great meditator, spiritual experience will dawn in your mind. In the presence of a bodhisattva, your compassion will expand, just as an ordinary log placed next to a log of sandalwood becomes saturated, little by little, with its fragrance. ॐ

93

Deception and lies deceive not only others,
but yourself as well;
People of Tingri, as witness take your own
conscience.

As Jetsun Milarepa said, "Finding nothing with which to reproach ourselves is the sign of the purity of our vows." Your own conscience is your best witness: it knows better than anyone the good and bad intentions you have had and the kind of actions you have committed. Whoever can say in good faith "I did my best" has a contented and serene mind.

Be the judge of your own faults, not those of others. Only a buddha knows others' deep motivations. Examine yourself to see whether you really live in accord with the Dharma. Emotionally driven devotion, outer respect for form, superficial compassion, and affected renunciation are not the attributes of an authentic practitioner. It is quite possible to live in complete contradiction to the Dharma while maintaining an irreproachable exterior. ๛

94

Delusion born from ignorance is the worst
disaster-bearing demon;
People of Tingri, hold fast to your vigilance
and mindfulness.

Ignorance is the original cause of our wandering in samsara. In fact, every being, even the smallest in-sect, is imbued with the Buddha-nature, as every seed of sesame is permeated with oil. But when beings are unaware of their true nature, the different forms that obscuration takes will cause them to suffer. That is what ignorance is.

Ignorance leads you to believe in the reality of your individual self and of phenomena. It leads to craving and repulsion, and to the stream of emotions that flows from them. This is how samsaric delusion sets in. An-chored in your mind, it devastates you, like an evil spirit that brings nothing but ruin and destruction. In his treatise *The Way of the Bodhisattva*,[12] Shantideva shows how the negative emotions have harmed us mercilessly throughout innumerable past lives. Therefore, it is desire and hatred we must oppose and not our ordinary enemies, who are themselves the unhappy victims of their passions.

No ordinary enemy, however cruel, can harm you beyond this lifetime. But the emotions are more formidable enemies, and have harmed you since time immemorial. They never stop encouraging you to act wrongly, and consequently cause you great suffering.

Now, with the help of your spiritual teacher, you can at last identify the true enemy. Brandish the sword of transcendent knowledge and annihilate the demon of attachment to "I" and to the reality of phenomena. ❧

95

*If you don't hold on to the three or five
poisons, the path is near;
People of Tingri, generate powerful
antidotes against them.*

All too often, our minds are governed by the five poisons—desire, hatred, ignorance, jealousy, and pride. Look at how hatred pushes people to kill each other, and nations to go to war. As long as you give free reign to your passions, they will dominate you. But when you analyze them carefully by following them back to their source, they vanish. They are like billowing storm clouds, imposing when seen from the outside but impalpable within. In short, afflictive emotions only have the power that you give to them. Rather than indulging in them again and again, be rid of them once and for all, and then liberation will be near at hand.

To succeed, you are going to have to summon up strong determination. Otherwise, your teacher's instructions will not be able to help you much, and your practice will lead nowhere. The teacher can guide you toward enlightenment, but cannot actually hurl you there like throwing a stone into the sky. He shows you the way, but it is up to you to follow it. Since your emotions are all-powerful, you must confront them with equally powerful antidotes. To get rid of a poisonous tree, you have to uproot it. Just pruning a few branches is not enough. In the same way, unless you uproot the emotions, they will just grow again, more vigorous than ever. ❧

96

If your perseverance has no strength, you
will not reach Buddhahood;
People of Tingri, make sure you don that
armor.

Diligence is the life force of spiritual practice. Shakyamuni became the Buddha by persevering for three aeons, and was reborn seventy-one times as a great king ready to sacrifice everything to receive the teachings of Dharma. The fruit of the merit he acquired through these efforts is the extraordinary power of his blessings.

It was also through constant effort that Jetsun Milarepa, the archetype of the determined practitioner, and all the other great realized masters were able to attain enlightenment. A meditator incapable of diligence, like a king without bodyguards, is an easy target for his enemies, laziness and the negative emotions.

The battle of liberation is about to be lost. Put on the armor of diligence without delay, and do battle with indolence. ❧

97

Habitual tendencies, being old acquaintances,
keep on coming back;
People of Tingri, don't go on following
the past.

Bad habits are strong and treacherous: strong because they are rooted in numerous past lifetimes, and treacherous because, beneath an engaging appearance, they can lead you to your ruin. While you are still a beginner in spiritual practice, your good habits, by contrast, are weak and timid.

Thanks to the kindness of your teacher, the buds of faith, enthusiasm, and perseverance have begun to sprout in your mind. But they are vulnerable to the inclemency of external circumstances. Like an inexperienced new recruit faced with a mercenary skilled in the martial arts, good habits are no match for bad ones. You are likely to continue as in the past, amassing goods, favoring those close to you while trying to

outdo your competitors, and so on, as did the genera-
tions before you. Thus you continue to be caught up
in activities as useless as they are endless.

If you lack vigilance and continue to succumb to
your bad habits, you may have received all the necessary instructions for attaining liberation, but you will
leave for the next life empty-handed and full of regret—like a merchant who carelessly sells off an heir-
loom of inestimable value for a trivial sum and then
goes bankrupt. Only through constant training will
you acquire stability in your practice and be able to
face your negative tendencies with confidence and
calm. ❧

98

If your understanding and realization are
weak, pray to your lord teacher,
People of Tingri, and deep meditation will
be born in you.

Sometimes you may get discouraged: your practice is not working, and you worry that it will never become stable. Nothing seems right, and you ask yourself whether you might not make swifter progress by changing to another practice. During these moments of doubt and hesitation, if a deep and yearning devotion for your teacher wells up from the depths of your heart, the obstacles that are impeding you will dissolve and your practice will be invigorated. Unshakable faith and devotion act like a magnifying glass that can concentrate the rays of the sun and easily kindle a heap of dried grass into flame.

Real progress on the path comes from the blessings of the guru, and these blessings are sparked by your devotion. Most of the great teachers of the past attained realization through devotion to their own gurus. For example, so great was the devotion of some of Gampopa's disciples that they realized the nature of mind simply by laying eyes on the Dagla Gampo mountain where he lived. ❧

99

If you aspire to happiness in the future,
accept your present trials,
People of Tingri—then Buddhahood is right
here just beside you.

W ho knows what kind of existence you will find
yourself in after this one? At present, you may
find it difficult to bear hunger, thirst, heat, and cold,
but these are minor difficulties compared with the sufferings you might face in future lives. From now on,
prepare for the unchanging bliss of liberation by practicing the Dharma.

If you ignore the prospect of future lives—or even
doubt that there are states of existence other than the
present one—and stick to ordinary goals, you will
waste your energy and all the precious potential of
human life. If you are sincerely devoted to achieving
it, Buddhahood is not far off. It is within you. It is

here and now, the primordial freshness of the present instant. It is the innate quality of each and every being.

The rich person who invests his capital increases his fortune, whereas the miser hoards it and it brings no benefit. The Buddha-nature is your natural treasure. It is up to you to make your fortune with it. ❧

100

*This old Indian master will not stay in
    Tingri, he will go away.
People of Tingri, it is now that you must
    clarify your doubts.*

Padampa, the old Indian *acharya,* warned his disciples that his days were numbered. You too should profit from the ephemeral meeting of teacher and disciple, to receive instruction and clear away your doubts. ॐ

101

I myself have practiced without distraction.
People of Tingri, you too should follow
my example.

Having abandoned all worldly activities, Padampa Sangye attained the ordinary and extraordinary accomplishments of the Adamantine Vehicle. He realized the ultimate nature of the mind and was able to benefit innumerable beings. He transcended all distraction and delusion. These hundred verses of advice are the expression of his inner realization. If you are seeking spiritual transformation, take the lives of the realized beings of the past as your model. If you follow the example of Padampa Sangye, there is no doubt that you can attain his level of realization. It all depends on your efforts. May that aspiration fill your mind!

Thus ends the spiritual testament of Padampa Sangye, his Hundred Verses of Advice to the people of Tingri.

NOTES

1. The teachings of the "Pacification of Suffering" (*zhi byed*) were introduced in Tibet by *Pa dam pa sangs rgyas*, d. 1117). They are based on the *Prajnaparamita*, the "Perfection of Transcendent Knowledge." Associated with these teachings are the practices of *chö* (*gcod*), which were introduced to Tibet by the great *yogini* Machik Labdron (*ma gcig lab sgron*, 1055–1153). The term *gcod* means "to cut." This practice aims at cutting the belief in the reality of the ego and of phenomena, as well as all other forms of attachment. One aspect of the practice consists of visualizing the offering of our body to four "guests" (*mgron po bzhi*), who are (1) the Three Jewels, the buddhas, and the bodhisattvas, who are worthy of our faith and respect; (2) the protectors of the doctrine, who are gifted with excellent qualities; (3) all living beings who merit our compassion; and (4) the spirits and negative forces to which we have karmic debts. This refers to the Eight Chariots of the Practice Lineages (Tib. *sgrub brgyud shing rta brgyad*): Nyingma, Kadam, Sakya, Kagyü, Shangpa Kagyü,

ZhiChey and Chod, Kalachakra or Jordug, and Orgyen Nyengyu.

2. This image comes from the life of Tibetan nomads, who conserve the butter they make in sheepskin containers. Sheep hairs may thus be found mixed with the butter, but when a hair is pulled out it carries no butter at all with it and leaves as its imprint an empty space where it had been.

3. The words of truth are the concise and powerful formulations of the fundamentals of Buddhism, of which the following are some examples:

> "Without committing the least
>   harmful act,
> Practice virtue perfectly,
> Completely mastering your mind:
> That is the teaching of the Buddha."

> "All things are transitory
> All passion is suffering,
> All phenomena are devoid of reality,
> Only nirvana is beyond suffering."

4. Offerings of water *torma*s (*chu gtor*) and burnt offerings (*gsur*) are made to the four "guests" (see note 1). Water tormas are made of pure water, mixed with milk and lumps of flour. The offering of the smoke from burnt food is accomplished by burning flour mixed with the "three white foods" (milk, butter, and cheese), and the "three sweet foods" (sugar, honey,

and molasses), as well as blessed substances. These offerings are accompanied by a visualization of the Buddha of Compassion, Avalokiteshvara, in the form of Kasarpani, and the recitation of his mantra, OM MANI PADME HUM HRI. There are many aspects of Avalokiteshvara, and Kasarpani is a common aspect found in the *kriya* tantras. From the perspective of the Mahayana sutras, Avalokiteshvara is often considered as one of the "eight bodhisattvas" who are the close spiritual heirs of the Buddha. From the perspective of the tantras, he is a fully enlightened wisdom deity belonging to the lotus family.

5. *Bardo* means "state of transition" and commonly designates the period of time that separates death from rebirth. More precisely, six bardos are spoken of:

+ The bardo of birth and life (*skyed gnas bar do*),
+ The bardo of meditative concentration (*bsam gtan bar do*),
+ The bardo of dream (*rmi lam bar do*),
+ The bardo of the moment of death (*'chi kha bar do*),
+ The bardo of the absolute nature (*chos nyid bar do*),
+ The bardo of the search for a new existence (*srid pa bar do*).

6. See note 2.

7. According to Buddhist cosmology, Mount Meru and the four continents, eight subcontinents, and seven oceans that surround them rest on a foundation of gold.

8. The eight worldly preoccupations are gain and loss, pleasure and pain, praise and blame, fame and obscurity.

9. The three *kaya*s, or bodies, are aspects or dimensions of Buddha-nature, which can be considered as one, two, three, four, or five bodies. The single body is Buddhahood. The two kayas are the dharmakaya, or absolute body, and the rupakaya, or body of form. The three kayas are the dharmakaya, or absolute body; the sambhogakaya, or body of perfect endowment; and the nirmanakaya, or manifest body. These last three correspond to the mind, speech, and body of a buddha and express themselves in the form of the five wisdoms.

10. Human life can be wasted in vain pursuits or devoted to progress toward enlightenment. A human life is only qualified as precious if it is endowed with the freedom to practice the Dharma and the other necessary and favorable conditions.

11. "Age of the five degenerations" or "five residues" (*dus snyigs ma lnga ldan*) translates the Sanskrit term *kaliyuga*. It is the age of dregs, when nothing remains but the debris of the perfection of the Golden Age. In particular, this dark age is characterized by the five degenerations: of life, of the environment, of metaphysical views, of the faculties of beings, and of their resistance to negative emotions.

12. See Shantideva, *The Way of the Bodhisattva,* trans. Padmakara Translation Group (Boston: Shambhala Publications, 1997).

GLOSSARY

ABSOLUTE TRUTH (Tib. *don dam bden pa*) The ultimate nature of the mind and the true status of all phenomena, the state beyond all conceptual constructs, which can be known only by primordial wisdom and in a manner that transcends duality; the way things are from the point of view of realized beings.

ACCOMPLISHMENT 1. (Tib. *dngos grub;* Skt. *siddhi*) The fruit wished for and obtained through the practice of the instructions. Common accomplishments can be simply supernatural powers, but in this book the term *accomplishment* almost always refers to the supreme accomplishment, which is enlightenment. 2. (Tib. *sgrub pa*) Term used in the context of the recitation of mantras.

ACTIONS (Tib. *las*) Actions resulting in the experience of happiness for others are defined as *positive* or virtuous; actions that give rise to suffering for others and oneself are described as *negative* or nonvirtuous. Every action, whether physical, mental, or verbal, is like a seed leading to a result that will be experienced in this life or in a future life.

ADAMANTINE VEHICLE (Skt. *Vajrayana*)   The corpus of teachings and practices based on the tantras and scriptures, that discourse upon the primordial purity of the mind. Also called the Vajrayana and the Secret Mantrayana.

AFFLICTIVE MENTAL FACTORS, or NEGATIVE EMOTIONS (Tib. *nyon mongs;* Skt. *klesha*)   All mental events that are born from ego-clinging disturb the mind and obscure it. The five principal afflictive mental factors, which are sometimes called "mental poisons," are attachment, hatred (or anger), ignorance, envy, and pride. They are the main causes of both immediate and long-term sufferings.

AGGREGATES, FIVE (Tib. *spung po;* Skt. *skandha;* lit. "heaps," "aggregates," or "events")   The five aggregates are the component elements of form, feeling, perception, conditioning factors, and consciousness. They are the elements into which the person may be analyzed without residue. When they appear together, the illusion of "self" is produced in the ignorant mind.

APPEARANCES (Tib. *snang ba*)   The world of outer phenomena. Although these phenomena seem to have a true reality, their ultimate nature is emptiness. The gradual transformation of our way of perceiving and understanding these phenomena corresponds to the various levels of the path to enlightenment.

ARHAT (Skt.; Tib. *dgra bcom pa)*   One who has vanquished the enemies of afflictive emotion and realized the nonexistence of a personal self, and who thus is forever free of the suffering of SAMSARA. Arhatship is the goal of Shravakayana, or HINAYANA, the Fundamental Vehicle.

AWARENESS, PURE (Tib. *rig pa*) The nondual ultimate nature of mind, which is totally free from delusion.

BARDO (Tibetan word meaning "intermediary state") This term most often refers to the state between death and subsequent rebirth. In fact, human experience encompasses six types of bardo: the bardo of the present life, the bardo of meditation, the bardo of dream, the bardo of dying, the luminous bardo of ultimate reality, and the bardo of becoming. The first three bardos unfold in the course of life. The second three refer to the death and rebirth process, which terminates at conception, the beginning of the subsequent existence.

BODHICHITTA (Tib. *byang chub kyi sems;* lit. "the mind of enlightenment") On the relative level, bodhichitta is the wish to attain Buddhahood for the sake of all beings, as well as to apply oneself to the practices necessary to accomplish it: the path of love, compassion, or the six paramitas, the six transcendent perfections, and so on. On the absolute level, it is direct insight into the ultimate nature.

BODHISATTVA (Tib. *byang chub sems dpa*) One who through COMPASSION strives to attain full enlightenment or Buddhahood for the sake of all beings.

BUDDHA (Tib. *sangs rgyas*) One who has completely eliminated (*sangs*) the two veils—the veil of emotional obscurations and the more subtle veil of cognitive obscurations (various degrees of dualistic concepts that prevent us from recognizing the true nature of things)—and who has fully developed (*rgyas*) the two wisdoms—the wisdom of knowing the ultimate nature of the mind and phenomena and the wisdom that knows phenomena in all their multiplicity. The Buddha Shakyamuni, the "historical" Buddha, is said to be the fourth of 1002 buddhas who will appear in our world during the present *kalpa*, while on a larger scale the sutras (especially those of the Mahayana) speak of countless buddhas of the past, present, and future, in all directions of space.

BUDDHA-NATURE (Tib. *bde gshegs snying po*) This is not an "entity" but rather the ultimate nature of mind, free from the veils of ignorance. Every sentient being has the potential to actualize this Buddha-nature by attaining perfect knowledge of the nature of mind. It is, in a way, the primordial goodness of sentient beings.

CLINGING, GRASPING, ATTACHMENT (Tib. *bdag 'dzin*) Its two main aspects are clinging to the true reality of the ego, and clinging to the reality of outer phenomena.

COMPASSION (Tib. *snying rje*) The wish to free all beings from suffering and the causes of suffering (negative actions and ignorance). It is complementary with *altruistic love* (the wish that all beings may find happiness and the causes of happiness), with *sympathetic joy* (rejoicing in others' qualities), and with *equanimity,* which extends the three former attitudes to all beings, whether friends, strangers, or enemies.

CONSCIOUSNESS (Tib. *rnam shes*) Buddhism distinguishes various levels of consciousness: gross, subtle, and extremely subtle.

The first corresponds to the activity of the brain. The second is what we intuitively call "consciousness." It is, among other things, the faculty of consciousness to know itself, investigate its own nature, and exert free will. The third aspect is the basic cognitive faculty of mind, free from mental images arising from perceptions of the external world, imagination, and memory. This pure awareness does not operate on the dual mode of subject and object, and does not involve discursive thoughts. These three types are not separate streams of consciousness, but lie at different increasingly deep levels. The gross and subtle levels both arise from the fundamental level, as opposed to the other way around as might be expected.

DHARMA (Tib. *chos*)   This Sanskrit term is usually used to indicate the doctrine of the historical Buddha. "The Dharma of transmission" refers to the corpus of verbal teachings, whether oral or written. "The Dharma of realization" refers to the spiritual qualities resulting from practicing these teachings.

DUALITY, DUALISTIC PERCEPTION (Tib. *gnyis 'dzin*)   The ordinary perception of unenlightened beings; the apprehension of phenomena in terms of subject (consciousness) and object (mental images and the outer world), and the belief in their true existence.

EGO, "I" (Tib. *bdag*)   Despite the fact that we are a ceaselessly transforming stream, interdependent with other beings and the whole world, we imagine that there exists in us an unchanging entity that characterizes us, one that we must protect and please. A thorough analysis of this ego reveals that it is only a fictitious mental construct.

EMPTINESS (Tib. *stong pa nyid*)   This is the ultimate nature of phenomena, due to their lack of inherent existence. The ultimate understanding of emptiness is accompanied by the spontaneous arising of boundless compassion for sentient beings.

ENLIGHTENMENT (Tib. *sangs rgyas*)   Synonymous with *Buddhahood*. It is the ultimate accomplishment of spiritual training, the point at which consummate inner wisdom is united with infinite compassion, resulting in a perfect understanding of the nature of mind and of phenomena: their relative mode of existence (the way they appear), and their ultimate nature (the way they are). Such understanding is the fundamental antidote to ignorance and, therefore, to suffering.

EXISTENCE, TRUE, INTRINSIC, OR REAL (Tib. *bden 'dzin*)   A state attributed to phenomena, suggesting that they could be independent objects existing in themselves, and having properties that belong to them intrinsically.

FIVE POISONS (Tib. *dug lnga*)   The five negative emotions: desire, hatred (including anger), ignorance, jealousy, and pride. See THREE POISONS.

FIVE WISDOMS (Tib. *ye shes lnga*)   Five aspects of the wisdom of Buddhahood: the wisdom of the absolute space, mirrorlike wisdom, the wisdom of equality, discriminating wisdom, and all-accomplishing wisdom.

FUNDAMENTAL VEHICLE (Tib. *theg dman*)   The fundamental system of Buddhist thought and practice deriving from the first turning of the wheel of Dharma and centering on the teachings on the Four Noble Truths (see SUFFERING) and the twelvefold chain of dependent arising (see INTERDEPENDENCE).

GAMPOPA (1079–1153). Also known as Dagpo Rinpoche; the most famous disciple of Jetsun Milarepa and the founder of the Kagyü monastic order.

GREAT PERFECTION (Tib. *rdzogs pa chen po;* Skt. *maha-sandhi*)   The summit of the nine vehicles and the ultimate view of the Nyingma school. "Perfection" means that the mind, in its nature, naturally contains all the qualities of the three bodies: its nature is emptiness, the dharmakaya; its natural expression is clarity, the sambhogakaya; and its compassion is all-encompassing, the nirmanakaya. See note 9 on page 180. See also VEHICLES, NINE GRADED.

GREAT VEHICLE (Tib. *theg pa chen po*)   Characteristic of Mahayana is the profound view of emptiness of the ego and all phenomena, coupled with universal compassion and the desire to deliver all beings from suffering and its causes. To this purpose, the goal of Mahayana is the attainment of the supreme enlightenment of Buddhahood, and its path consists of the practice of the six *paramita*s.

HABITUAL TENDENCIES (Tib. *bag chags*)   Habitual patterns of thought, speech, or action that have been created by what one has done in past lives.

HINAYANA   See FUNDAMENTAL VEHICLE.

IGNORANCE (Tib. *ma rig pa*)   An erroneous way to conceive of beings and things, by attributing to them an existence that is real, independent, solid, and intrinsic.

ILLUSION (Tib. *'khrul pa*)   All ordinary perception deformed by ignorance.

IMPERMANENCE (Tib. *mi rtag pa*)   Gross impermanence pertains to visible change; subtle impermanence reflects the fact that nothing can remain identical to itself, even for the shortest conceivable moment.

INTERDEPENDENCE, OR "DEPENDENT ORIGINATION" (Tib. *rten cing 'brel bar 'byung ba*)   A fundamental element of Buddhist teaching according to which phenomena are understood not as discretely existent entities, but as the coincidence of interdependent conditions.

JETSUN MILAREPA (1040–1123)   Tibet's great yogi and poet, whose biography and spiritual songs are among the best-loved works in Tibetan Buddhism. He attained Buddhahood in one lifetime.

KALPA (Skt.; Tib. *bskal pa*)   A great *kalpa,* which corresponds to a cycle of formation and destruction of a universe, is divided into eighty intermediate kalpas. An intermediate kalpa is composed of one small kalpa during which the span of life increases, and one small kalpa during which it decreases.

KARMA (Tib. *las*)   This Sanskrit word (literally "action") refers to the law of cause and effect as related to our thoughts, words, and behavior. According to the Buddha's teachings, beings' destinies, joys, sufferings, and perceptions of the universe are due neither to chance nor to the will of some all-powerful entity. They are the result of previous actions. In the same way, the future of beings is determined by the positive or negative quality of their current actions. Distinction is made between collective karma, which defines our general perception of the world, and individual karma, which determines our personal experiences.

LAMA (Tib. *bla ma;* Skt. *guru*)   1. Spiritual teacher, explained as the contraction of *bla na med pa*, or "nothing superior." 2. A term often loosely used for Buddhist monks or yogis in general.

LIBERATION (Tib. *thar pa*)   To be free from suffering and the cycle of existences. This state is not yet the attainment of full Buddhahood.

LOWER REALMS (Tib. *ngan song*)   The hells, the realms of *preta*s (tortured spirits) and of animals.

MAHAYANA   See GREAT VEHICLE.

MEDITATION (Tib. *sgom*)   A process of familiarization with a new perception of phenomena. Distinction is made between analytical meditation and contemplative meditation. The object of the former could be a point to be studied (for instance, the notion of impermanence) or a quality that we wish to develop (such as love and compassion); the latter allows us to recognize the ultimate nature of the mind and to remain within the realization of this nature, which lies beyond conceptual thought.

MERIT (Tib. *bsod nams;* Skt. *punya*)   Positive energy generated by wholesome actions of body, speech, and mind.

MIDDLE WAY (Tib. *dbu ma;* Skt. *madhyamika*)   The teachings on emptiness first expounded by Nagarjuna and considered to be the basis of the Secret Mantrayana (see also

ADAMANTINE VEHICLE). "Middle" means it is beyond the points of view of the two extremes of *nihilism* on the one hand and the belief in the reality of phenomena (*eternalism* or *materialism*) on the other.

MIND (Tib. *sems; see also* CONSCIOUSNESS)   In Buddhist terms, the ordinary condition of the mind is characterized by ignorance and delusion. A succession of conscious instants gives it an appearance of continuity. On the absolute level, the mind has three aspects: emptiness, clarity (the ability to know all things), and spontaneous compassion.

NIRVANA (Skt.; Tib. *myang 'da 'sdas*) Literally, the state beyond suffering. This term refers to any of several levels of enlightenment, depending on whether our viewpoint is from the Fundamental Vehicle or the Great Vehicle. See FUNDAMENTAL VEHICLE, GREAT VEHICLE.

OBSCURATIONS (Tib. *sgrib pa;* Skt. *avarana*)   Factors that veil one's BUDDHA-NATURE.

PATH (Tib. *lam*)   The spiritual training that allows one to free oneself from the cycle of existence (see SAMSARA) and then reach the state of Buddhahood.

PHENOMENA (Tib. *snang ba*)   What appears to the mind through sensory perceptions and mental events.

REBIRTH, REINCARNATION (Tib. *skyes*)   The successive states that are experienced by the flow of consciousness, and which are punctuated by death, bardo, and birth (see BARDO).

REFUGE   (1) Tib. *skyabs yul.* The object in which one takes refuge. (2) Tib. *skyabs 'gro.* The practice of taking refuge. See also THREE JEWELS.

RELATIVE TRUTH (Tib. *kun rdzob bden pa,* lit. "all-concealing truth") This refers to phenomena in the ordinary sense, which, on the level of ordinary experience, are perceived as real and separate from the mind and which thus conceal its true nature.

SAMSARA (Skt.; Tib. *'gro drug*) Six modes of existence caused and dominated by a particular mental poison: the realms of hell (hatred and anger), of *preta*s or hungry ghosts (miserliness), of animals (ignorance), of humans (desire), of *asura*s or demigods (jealousy), and of gods (pride). They correspond to deluded perceptions produced by beings' karma and are apprehended as real.

SUFFERING (Tib. *sdug bsngal*) The entire gamut of unsatisfactory experience that characterizes the six realms of samsara. In his first teaching, the Buddha made suffering the focus of the Four Noble Truths, of which the first (the truth of suffering) identifies suffering as omnipresent in samsara; the second (the truth of the origin of suffering) identifies as its causes the negative emotions and actions resulting from them; the third (the truth of the path) affirms that suffering can be brought to a complete cessation; and the fourth (the truth of the cessation of suffering) sets out the path of spiritual training through which the causes of suffering can be eliminated in order to bring it to that very cessation.

SUTRA (Tib. *mdo*) The words of Buddha Shakyamuni, which were transcribed by his disciples.

THOUGHTS, DISCURSIVE (Tib. *rnam par thog pa*) An ordinary linking together of thoughts conditioned by ignorance and relative reality.

THREE JEWELS (Tib. *dkon mchog gsum;* Skt. *triratna*) The Buddha, the Dharma, and the Sangha. These are the three objects of refuge for someone who enters on the Buddhist path. The Buddha is the guide, the Dharma is the path, and the Sangha (all those who practice the Buddhist teachings) the companions on the path.

THREE POISONS (Tib. *dug gsum*) The three negative emotions of desire, hatred, and ignorance.

VAJRAYANA (Skt.; Tib. *rdo rje theg pa*) See ADAMANTINE VEHICLE.

VEHICLES, NINE GRADED (Tib. *theg pa rim pa dgyu*) The three sutric vehicles of the Sravakas, the Pratyekabuddhas, and the Bodhisattvas, followed by the six vehicles of Kriya, Upa, Yoga, Mahayoga, Anuyoga, and Atiyoga tantras. They can also be grouped into three vehicles: Hinayana, which comprises the first two, Mahayana (the third), and Vajrayana (the last six).

VIEW, MEDITATION, AND ACTION (Tib. *lta, sgom, spyod pa*) The vision of emptiness must be integrated into our mind through meditation, and is expressed in turn in altruistic actions and ultimate enlightened activities.

WISDOM 1. (Tib. *shes rab;* Skt. *prajna*) The ability to discern correctly, usually with the particular sense of the understanding of emptiness. 2. (Tib. *ye shes;* Skt. *jnana*) The primordial and nondual knowing aspect of the nature of the mind. See FIVE WISDOMS.

Printed in the United States
by Baker & Taylor Publisher Services